What Have You Harvested Lately?

Lori Gracey

Printed in the United States of America
Lightning Press
Totowa, New Jersey

Unless otherwise noted, Scripture quotations taken from the *Holy Bible*, New American Standard Bible ®, Copyright © 1960, 1962, 1963, 1968, 1971, 1972, 1973, 1975, 1977, 1995 by The Lockman Foundation. All rights reserved.

Additional Scripture quotations are from the *Holy Bible*, English Standard Version, Copyright © 2001 by Crossway Bibles, a division of Good News Publishers. All rights reserved.

Cover artwork © Rosa Chavez, Artist, Courtesy of Canadian Art Prints, Inc. *Grapes on Blue Wagon.*

Cover design by Ed McConnell Design, Tulsa, Oklahoma.

Gracey, Lori.
    What Have You Harvested Lately?
    ISBN 0-6152-7796-9
    1. Spiritual growth – Christianity. I Title

Dedication

To my parents, Glenn and Ann, who taught me about reaping harvests from the soil and the soul.

Acknowledgements

Many people have contributed to the production of this book. In particular I wish to express my gratitude to:

Bodie Thoene for answering my countless questions about book publishing. Without her guidance, I'd probably be running copies down at the copy shop right now.

Larry Landis for his expertise in reviewing, editing and helping with the layout of the book. When I need the detail work done and done right, I call Larry.

Al Poncel who provided the final motivation I needed to finish this project in time for it to be used for the Adult Sunday School classes at church.

Mary Spreiter, my Greek professor, for instructing me in the beauty and subtle detail of the Greek language. Thank you also for pointing me to the Biblos Greek font!

Larry and Mary Ehrlich for being wonderful home group leaders and tour guides of Israel. You've made the Hebrew roots of our faith indelibly vivid and real to me.

Linda Noble, Catherine Pasion-Fox, Ed McConnell, Daniele Holland and Paul Balinski for the particular assistance each of you provided on this project.

The readers of BranchesInTheVine.org who were the first to read and comment on this project. Thank you each one.

And certainly most of all, the True Vine from whom all great harvests come.

CONTENTS

Cultivating a Harvest

How blessed is everyone who fears the LORD, who walks in His ways. When you shall eat of the fruit of your hands, you will be happy and it will be well with you.

(Psalm 128:1-2)

Along the Valley Road

Extending north and then west through the valley, the road winds languidly, a ribbon ensconcing manicured rows of vines. Stately oaks, occasional orchards, and ancient groves of redwoods punctuate the path, only to be followed by unencumbered vistas of verdant hillsides.

Continuing along the valley road, the glow of sunrise hints its arrival over your shoulder. Mist floats dreamily in small vales tucked like memories rising from a warm, downy quilt. It is morning, but not quite, when sleeping and waking bid their final farewells.

Row upon row of stately vines stand at rapt attention, awaiting the dawn of their harvest. Their brilliant hues of red, gold, and dappled green draw your eye to the autumn rainbow of the fields. A latticework of grizzled vines, twining branches, and richly colored leaves provides a brilliant backdrop to their prize. Darkened into the shadowy recesses of each row are the heavily laden clusters of fruit.

Ascending the road to meet the sun, you reach the crest of a damp, wooded hillside only just emerging from the morning haze. Looking toward the valley floor, you behold the first fingers of golden sunlight reaching across the valley to caress the bounty of the harvest.

Breathing in the beauty of the panorama, your senses are greeted by the muskiness of forest duff, suffused with a hint of drifting lavender. The cacophony of earthy aromas is shrouded with the robustness of rich brown earth and an ethereal whiff of ripeness, hinting of rot that will not be held at bay for long.

It is time. All the efforts of preparing the soil, tending the rows, removing the weeds, watering, training, pruning, and cultivating have brought about this moment. It is the crucial interval when all that has gone before pales in contrast to the wealth accumulating on the vines.

Following the harvest, tables will be graced with skillfully crafted wines. Fruits of the vineyard will compliment coffee and croissant alongside morning papers. Meals and desserts will be accented with the crisp crunch of slivered almonds. Perhaps a crab stuffed filet of sole will be encrusted with toasted almonds, complimented by a dry Sauvignon Blanc, and completed with a decadent cheesecake draped with the tanginess of blackberry preserves.

Anticipating the opulent rewards of the harvest, with brimming anticipation you greet your host. This is the one responsible for the bounty of the fields. This is the one responsible for preparing the soil before planting, for tending the crops throughout the growing season, and now for conducting the harvest.

The Incongruous Gardner

Pleasantries exchanged, you inquire as to when the work of harvesting the various crops begins. Upon hearing the grower's reply, you wonder if your question was understood, for the response seemed to indicate that there would be no harvest. Rephrasing the question, you are unimaginably nonplussed by the reply.

There will be no harvest.

Taking in your confused expression, your host explains. It is true that great effort has gone into producing the crops evident across the panorama of the valley. Years have been invested. Countless hours of labor have been exerted. And isn't this enough? Why should the scene be spoiled by harvesting the fruit that is awaiting the picking?

The incongruous gardener insists that the mere appearance of bounty is enough. There is no need for anything more.

Perplexed, you inquire concerning the precarious climax that approaches with the advance of the fall. It is autumn, after all, and soon what remains in the field will begin its return to the earth. Isn't such a loss of produce a wasteful extravagance? What of those who could benefit from the harvest?

Blithely insistent that harvesting is too great a nuisance, your host strolls forward in search of a better vantage from which to observe the wealth of the fields. It is no matter what benefit such a harvest might bring to others. This crop is meant solely for the gardener's pleasure. It is to be looked upon for its pastoral beauty. Its fragrance is to be enjoyed for its soothing tranquility. But this expanse of grape and almond, of berry and citrus lying tenuously within reach is meant only to gratify the sensual appetite of the grower, not the palate.

Preposterous! Unthinkable! Or is it?

Spiritual Cultivation

Spiritually, each one of us is meant to cultivate a garden. We are responsible for preparing the soil, for attending to the germination of strong and fruitful foliage. We must water and weed, prune and train, fertilize and till. We must nurture our gardens so that our harvest is bountiful.

And what is it that we are to harvest in this well-tended garden? Crops of love, an abundance of joy, peace by the bushel, and patience by the cartful are to make up our harvest. The rows of our vineyards, gardens, and orchards should overflow with kindness, goodness, faithfulness, gentleness, and self-control.

For whom are we raising such bountiful spiritual produce? We raise such crops in obedience to our Lord's command and we do so to bring blessings to others. If we cultivate without harvesting or harvest only to benefit ourselves, we are as senseless as the grower who left grape, almond, berry and citrus to rot on the vine.

Perhaps this admonition is presumptuous? It is presupposed on the conviction that there is indeed a Lord and that the Father of this Lord is the Vinedresser. If there is no Vinedresser then there is no Lord, which leads to the conclusion that there is no one but one's self for whom crops should be produced.

But, if your view of the world begins with the conviction that there is a divine Vinedresser and a Son who is Lord of this garden called Earth, then your responsibilities concerning the production of fruit are quite different. And indeed there is a divine Vinedresser just as Jesus said in John 15:1, "I am the true vine, and My Father is the Vinedresser."

Accepting this fact, what Christ has to say next becomes quite compelling. "Every branch in Me that does not bear fruit, He takes away; and every branch that bears fruit, He prunes it so that it may bear more fruit" (John 15:2). This quite obviously begs the question: Will you bear fruit?

If you choose to produce fruit, you'll undergo whatever pruning is required to make you the most productive. If it's not self-evident, pruning requires that bits and pieces be trimmed away. To put it plainly, the deadwood in the life of one intending to bear fruit will be cut off and tossed out.

Of course there is an alternative to all of this cutting and trimming. One can choose not to bear fruit. However, this still involves cutting. But whereas pruning cuts away bits and pieces that inhibit the full potential of fruitful branches, unfruitful branches are fully excised. In the end, they are burned up in the fire.

The Vinedresser's Fields

The divine Vinedresser has made a way for each one of us to propagate the fruit of his fields. If we elect to serve the Lord of the Vinedresser's fields, we will be pruned and trained into beautifully productive branches. Jesus describes it this way:

Abide in Me, and I in you. As the branch cannot bear fruit of itself unless it abides in the vine, so neither can you unless you abide in Me. I am the vine, you are the branches; he who abides in Me and I in him, he bears much fruit, for apart from Me you can do nothing (John 15:4-5).

The Greek verb translated in English as either *abide* or *remain* is *meno* (μένω). English has also derived such words as *manse* and *mansion* from meno. The verb meno carries the connotation of remaining permanently, dwelling, or taking up residency. This is the manner by which we are to remain in Christ. We are to take up permanent residency in him. Horticulturally speaking, we are to be grafted into him with the same permanency that a grape-producing vine is grafted into an ancient and established rootstock. Remove the grafted branch and it withers while the rootstock continues to flourish robust and strong.

Will you choose to abide in Christ with this level of permanency? Will you choose to acknowledge his Father, the Vinedresser, who is our Creator? Will you choose to produce the fruit of the Father's harvest so that the lives around you are touched by the benefits of his character, his nature, his life? Or will you choose to be as the foolish gardener who allowed his bountiful crops to rot, profiting no one?

The abundance of abiding in Christ and bearing the fruit of the Father's harvest exceeds all imagination. Abiding, remaining, residing and staying in Christ will change your life and the lives of all who are blessed to partake of the harvest that only Christ can cultivate through you.

For to everyone who has, more shall be given, and he will have an abundance; (Matthew 25:29).

What have you harvested lately?

1. How well am I abiding in Christ?

2. What bits and pieces in my life need to be pruned so that my harvest of spiritual fruit increases?

3. Who would be blessed if I began producing more spiritual fruit?

4. What have I harvested lately?

Paul's Spiritual Harvest

For you were called to freedom, brethren; only do not turn your freedom into an opportunity for the flesh, but through love serve one another. For the whole Law is fulfilled in one word, in the statement, "You shall love your neighbor as yourself." But if you bite and devour one another, take care that you are not consumed by one another.

But I say, walk by the Spirit, and you will not carry out the desire of the flesh. For the flesh sets its desire against the Spirit, and the Spirit against the flesh; for these are in opposition to one another, so that you may not do the things that you please. But if you are led by the Spirit, you are not under the Law.

Now the deeds of the flesh are evident, which are: immorality, impurity, sensuality, idolatry, sorcery, enmities, strife, jealousy, outbursts of anger, disputes, dissensions, factions, envying, drunkenness, carousing, and things like these, of which I forewarn you, just as I have forewarned you, that those who practice such things will not inherit the kingdom of God.

But the Fruit of the Spirit is love, joy, peace, patience, kindness, goodness, faithfulness, gentleness, self-control; against such things there is no law (Galatians 5:13-23).

Ancient Rootstock

But the Fruit of the Spirit is love, joy, peace, patience, kindness, goodness, faithfulness, gentleness, self-control; against such things there is no law (Galatians 5:22-23).

Then a shoot will spring from the stem of Jesse, And a branch from his roots will bear fruit (Isaiah 11:1).

Agricultural Ingenuity

Vineyards are interesting feats of agricultural ingenuity. Take for instance the fact that a significant percentage of wine grapes grown in North America are produced on rootstock that is different than the harvested grape variety. Why? Well, it all has to do with the quality of the fruit produced and the ability of the plant to produce it. Left alone, most grape vines will produce grapes in even the most neglected conditions. But the quality of the grapes will be pretty much useless unless properly cultivated.

Then there is the problem of grape phylloxera, a tiny aphid-like insect that feeds on certain types of grape roots, stunting the growth of vines or killing them completely. The most effective means of preventing this destructive infestation, or eradicating it once it starts, is to change the rootstock to a variety resistant to the pest.

What graphic insight this provides into the words of Christ when he says that he is the Vine and we are merely the branches.

> *I am the vine, you are the branches; he who abides in Me and I in him, he bears much fruit, for apart from Me you can do nothing* (John 15:5).

Vintner and vineyardist know that what is casually referred to as merely a grapevine is in reality far more complex. First, there is the rootstock from which the vine trunk grows. It is to this vine trunk that fruit-bearing branches are grafted in order to produce the desired variety of grapes. Thus when Jesus called himself the Vine, he was essentially saying, "I'm the Rootstock and Vine Trunk, and you are the grafted-in, fruit-bearing branches."

Jesus is the Root and Vine that is resistant to the phylloxera known as sin. Apart from him, growing on our own carnal root, we can do nothing but produce worthless fruit and eventually wither away. But once we are grafted into him, we are able to resist our innate sinfulness and are capable of producing fruit that far exceeds our natural abilities. Therefore, just as a vine branch abides in the rootstock's vine trunk, when we abide in Christ, we become capable of producing quality fruit.

Spiritual Varietals

The metaphorical comparison does not stop there. Just as we see Christ in the rootstock and ourselves in the branches, the grape varieties are comparable to spiritual gifts.

Now there are varieties of gifts, but the same Spirit. And there are varieties of ministries, and the same Lord. There are varieties of effects, but the same God who works all things in all persons. But to each one is given the manifestation of the Spirit for the common good.

For to one is given the word of wisdom through the Spirit, and to another the word of knowledge according to the same Spirit; to another faith by the same Spirit, and to another gifts of healing by the one Spirit, and to another the effecting of miracles, and to another prophecy, and to another the distinguishing of spirits, to another various kinds of tongues, and to another the interpretation of tongues. But one and the same Spirit works all these things, distributing to each one individually just as He wills (I Corinthians 12:4-11).

Just as in a vineyard there are typically different varieties of grapes being grown, so we too are each one distinguished by our particular spiritual gifts. But having differing gifts does not equate to bearing different fruit. A Cabernet is distinguishable from a Chardonnay, just as a prophet is distinguishable from a worker of miracles. But the fact remains that the grape vine produces grapes. Likewise, while being distinct in our gifts, we are to produce the same Fruit of the Spirit. Prophet or miracle worker, the Fruit of the Spirit should be fully evident in the manifestations of our unique gifts.

So, we are branches grafted into Jesus Christ, the true Rootstock, who was prophesied by Isaiah to be the root of Jesse.

> *Then in that day the nations will resort to the root of Jesse, who will stand as a signal for the peoples; and His resting place will be glorious* (Isaiah 11:10).

Once grafted into Christ, we are to produce the Fruit of the Spirit regardless of our particular grape variety or spiritual giftedness. These spiritual fruit are nine in number according to the Apostle Paul who wrote under the inspiration of the Holy Spirit.

> *But the Fruit of the Spirit is love, joy, peace, patience, kindness, goodness, faithfulness, gentleness, self-control; against such things there is no law* (Galatians 5:22-23).

And so we are provided with our spiritual produce list. These are the traits that should be evident in our lives. It is for the purpose of bearing this fruit that we are grafted into Jesus Christ. This is the harvest that yields the double portion. For not only are our own lives enriched by such bounty, our yield should equally bring blessings and enrichment to every person whose life we touch.

Is the waitress at the diner refreshed by your gentleness and peace? Is the clerk at the copy center encouraged by your patience and kindness? How has your neighbor's life been enriched by your faithfulness and self-control? What does your harvest reveal?

Grafted-in Resistence

Paul goes on to explain that when a follower of Christ surrenders their personal will and desires and gives themselves fully to Christ, the weak vulnerabilities of the natural self fade into obscurity. The same is the case for vinestock that is grafted into rootstock resistant to life-destroying parasites. The hardiness of the Rootstock overcomes the susceptibility to the phylloxera of sin.

Now those who belong to Christ Jesus have crucified the flesh with its passions and desires (Galatians 5:24).

It is my heartfelt desire that this book challenge each one of us who follow Christ to examine our lives daily and see if we are bearing the right kind of fruit. Jesus assures us of a fact with which all farmers are intimately acquainted: a plant is identifiable by the fruit it produces. What have you harvested lately?

For each tree is known by its own fruit. For men do not gather figs from thorns, nor do they pick grapes from a briar bush (Luke 6:44).

Of course you don't want to be a briar bush. But if you discover that you are producing more carnal fruit than the Fruit of the Spirit, you would do well to heed Paul's warning. He warns that such individuals will not inherit the kingdom of God. Consider this list of carnal fruit that the briar bush bears:

Now the deeds of the flesh are evident, which are: immorality, impurity, sensuality, idolatry, sorcery, enmities, strife, jealousy, outbursts of anger, disputes, dissensions, factions, envying, drunkenness, carousing, and things like these, of which I forewarn you, just as I have forewarned you, that those who practice such things will not inherit the kingdom of God (Galatians 5:19-21).

Notice that the list of carnal fruit is much longer than that of spiritual fruit. This is similar to the ratio of weeds to flowers in a typical flowerbed. For every blossom one hopes to grow, a half dozen different weeds spring up to choke out the blooms. It is only through consistent grooming of the flowerbed that the noxious weeds are eventually overcome.

However, any backyard gardener will tell you that even then, when it appears every unwanted chard of green is removed, one must keep a wary eye to pluck away the weeds that inevitably return. Gardens, like our lives, must be guarded and tended daily. Such is not the vocation of anyone who is passive or unobservant.

Paul's admonition for us to produce good fruit or suffer the consequence harkens to Jesus' warning in John's Gospel. Our Lord cautioned us that branches failing to produce wholesome fruit are cut from the vine and thrown into the fire.

> *If anyone does not abide in Me, he is thrown away as a branch and dries up; and they gather them, and cast them into the fire and they are burned* (John 15:6).

Fruit Inspection

Just as planting a flat of petunias and then neglecting them fails to produce a beautiful flower garden, so only believing in Christ and never acting on that belief yields a desolate life. It is not enough to merely believe in Christ Jesus, for even the demons believe and are in terror as a result.

> *You believe that God is one. You do well; the demons also believe, and shudder* (James 2:19).

Believing without following results in a sickly grapevine that produces miserable fruit and tainted wine. It is the same as planting a flowerbed and never returning to water, weed, or tend it. It is not acceptable to live life content with such substandard produce. To persist in a lifestyle of sinful behavior is to live in rejection of the Lordship of Christ.

Does this mean that Christians never struggle and stumble into sin? Do the weeds of sin never creep in? No, Christians certainly do struggle with sin. Romans 3:23 clearly states that we are all sinners; "for all have sinned and fall short of the glory of God".

But stumbling into sin is far different than abiding in a lifestyle of sin. Even the most ardently tended vineyard may have an outbreak of destructive organisms from phylloxera to weeds, from mold to mildew. If these blights are left unchecked, the sickness spreads and soon the entire crop and even the vineyard itself is consumed.

Likewise, the disease of sin must be guarded against and removed whenever it is discovered in one's life. When discovered, the weeds of sin are quickly dealt with by following John's instruction in his first epistle.

If we confess our sins, He is faithful and righteous to forgive us our sins and to cleanse us from all unrighteousness (1 John 1:9).

Our challenge is to continually hold ourselves accountable to the Word of God and the conviction of the Holy Spirit. We must inspect our fruit to see that it satisfies God's standards and not merely our own. Additionally, we must lovingly hold one another accountable to such standards just as Jesus instructs us in Matthew's Gospel:

If your brother sins, go and show him his fault in private; if he listens to you, you have won your brother (Matthew 18:15).

In the following chapters, we will consider each of the nine Fruit of the Spirit. We will examine what each one entails and consider what they should look like our in daily lives. It is my prayer that each of us is challenged to examine our lives, and to lay aside our sinful desires so that we commit more consistently to produce godly spiritual fruit in all that we say and do. By God's grace, his Word has the power to transform us so that our spiritual harvest abounds to his glory.

> *And do not be conformed to this world, but be transformed by the renewing of your mind, so that you may prove what the will of God is, that which is good and acceptable and perfect* (Romans 12:2).

What have you harvested lately?

1. Who have I refreshed with my gentleness and peace?

2. Who has been encouraged by my patience and kindness?

3. How has my neighbor been enriched by my faithfulness and self-control?

4. What have I harvested lately?

An Uncompromising Crop

The Fruit of Love

But the Fruit of the Spirit is love, joy, peace, patience, kindness, goodness, faithfulness, gentleness, self-control; against such things there is no law (Galatians 5:22-23).

In this is love, not that we loved God, but that He loved us and sent His Son to be the propitiation for our sins (1 John 4:10).

Unconditional Affection

Paul begins his spiritual produce list in Galatians chapter five with the Fruit of Love. Unfortunately, in our modern world, this word, *love*, has been widely applied to a myriad of things. A husband loves his wife. Teenagers love their cars. A mother loves her children. An executive loves the profit made on a business deal. But few, if any, of these depict the love of which Paul speaks in his letter to the Galatian churches.

Paul uses the Greek word *agape* (ἀγάπη) when he speaks of Christian love. Agape is unconditional and uncompromising love extended to another person not based on any merit of their own. In addition to agape, Greek uses three other words that are translated into English by the single word, love.

Besides unconditional agape love, there is *eros* (ἔρως)—passionate, sensual desire from which we have the word erotic. We also have *phileo* (φιλέω) dispassionate, virtuous, brotherly affection from which Philadelphia, the city of brotherly love, is derived. And finally there is *storge* (στόργη)—the simplest of loves. C.S. Lewis describes storge as natural affection such as that of parents toward their offspring.

Of the four choices available to him, Paul indicated that it is agape love that followers of Christ are to exhibit in their lives. This is the love he spoke of in 1 Corinthians 13, universally known as the Love Chapter. In that passage, as in Galatians 5, no other form of love would sufficiently instruct us in what manner of care and affection we are to show to others. Only the purity and selflessness of agape suffices.

It is agape love that provides the basis for the other eight Fruit of the Spirit. Without agape love, it would be impossible to exhibit these other traits. But to say that agape love is unconditional is not to say that it is without boundaries.

True love affirms justice and rejects injustice; it upholds truth and renounces falsehood; it is neither passive nor aggressive, but instead expresses itself with calm assertion. To further examine the subtleties of agape love, we'll consider the source of agape, in addition to both its affirming and intolerant aspects.

Seeking the Source

Discovering the source of love is as elementary as reading the following brief passage from First John in which the term agape is exclusively used.

Beloved, let us love one another, for love is from God; and everyone who loves is born of God and knows God. The one who does not love does not know God, for God is love (1 John 4:7-8).

Simply put, John tells us that love is from God because God is love, and that everyone who knows God will love others. Without God, there could be no love. It is no wonder then that the greatest commandment is to love God unconditionally. Indeed, this love for our Creator is the foundation of our faith.

It is because of its centrality to our faith that Moses directs the righteous to focus on loving God. The entire Law is succinctly summarized in the words of the Jewish affirmation, the Shema, from Deuteronomy and Numbers. Observant Jews confess this ancient creed of faith to this very day. The complete text of the Shema is found in Deuteronomy 6:4-9, 11:13-21, and Numbers 15:37-41. Proclaiming the centrality of the first Commandment, the Shema begins:

Hear, O Israel! The LORD is our God, the LORD is one! You shall love the LORD your God with all your heart and with all your soul and with all your might (Deuteronomy 6:4-5).

It is these initial verses that Christ refers to when asked to identify which is the greatest commandment. In each of the synoptic Gospels, our Lord affirms that we must first love God with true agape love.

And He said to him, "You shall love the LORD your God with all your heart, and with all your soul, and with all your mind" (Matthew 22:37).

And you shall love the LORD your God with all your heart, and with all your soul, and with all your mind, and with all your strength (Mark 12:30).

And he answered, "You shall love the LORD your God with all your heart, and with all your soul, and with all your strength, and with all your mind; and your neighbor as yourself" (Luke 10:27).

Jesus refers to Leviticus when he notes that we are to love our neighbors just as we love God; with pure, selfless, agape love.

You shall not take vengeance, nor bear any grudge against the sons of your people, but you shall love your neighbor as yourself; I am the LORD (Leviticus 19:18).

Love for other people naturally stems from one's love of God. If this command to love is fully kept, one would truly be able to keep all the commandments, for each one grows out of pure agape love.

This is the great and foremost commandment. The second is like it, "You shall love your neighbor as yourself." On these two commandments depend the whole Law and the Prophets (Matthew 22.38-40).

Owe nothing to anyone except to love one another; for he who loves his neighbor has fulfilled the law. For this, "You shall not commit adultery, you shall

*not murder, you shall not steal, you shall not covet,"
and if there is any other commandment, it is summed
up in this saying, "You shall love your neighbor as
yourself." Love does no wrong to a neighbor;
therefore love is the fulfillment of the law*
(Romans 13:8-10).

Just as love encapsulates the commandments, it likewise encompasses the Fruit of the Spirit. Paul begins his Love Chapter by outlining the attributes of agape love.

*Love is patient, love is kind and is not jealous; love
does not brag and is not arrogant, does not act
unbecomingly; it does not seek its own, is not
provoked, does not take into account a wrong
suffered, does not rejoice in unrighteousness, but
rejoices with the truth; bears all things, believes all
things, hopes all things, endures all things. Love
never fails* (1 Corinthians 13:4-8a).

True agape love affirms patience, kindness, justice, confidence, and hope, all with perseverance. At the same time, this love is intolerant of jealousy, boasting, arrogance, rudeness, selfishness, irritability, resentfulness, and injustice. Paul asserts that agape love never falls into a state of ruin or decay. And how could it, since God—who is forever eternal—is the source of agape love?

Grounded in Love

One way to appreciate the extensive impact of love on spiritual fruit is to compare love to the soil of a vineyard.

The type of soil in which a grapevine is planted directly affects the quality and character of the fruit produced by the vine. In his *Complete Guide to Wine Tasting and Wine Cellars*, Michael Broadbent notes that "the best wines are made from vines grown in uncompromising terrain."

Broadbent goes on to describe such terrain as mineral rich soil inclusive of some mixture of rock, gravel, slate, or large pebbles. In these soils, the vine must struggle to extend its roots deep enough to tap into the moisture necessary for growth. While this struggle may result in a smaller crop than vines planted in loose, moist soil, what it lacks in quantity, it greatly makes up for in quality.

It is tempting to draw a comparison between the terrain of these quality-producing vineyards and Christ's parable of the sower in Matthew chapter 13:

> *Behold, the sower went out to sow; and as he sowed, some seeds fell beside the road, and the birds came and ate them up. Others fell on the rocky places, where they did not have much soil; and immediately they sprang up, because they had no depth of soil. But when the sun had risen, they were scorched; and because they had no root, they withered away. Others fell among the thorns, and the thorns came up and choked them out. And others fell on the good soil and yielded a crop, some a hundredfold, some sixty, and some thirty* (Matthew 13:3-8).

But didn't Christ say that the rocky soil produced shallow roots that grew quickly and then withered just as fast? Yes, he did. But this isn't the same type of rocky soil vineyards are grown upon. The rocky soil of the parable is impenetrable stone slab covered by minimal top soil (πετρώδη, solid like a rock or stone).

Conversely, the good soil of the vineyard is rocky, yet rich in minerals and top soil; rocky, yet porous enough to filter life-giving water; rocky, yet malleable enough to allow roots to go deep and drink in the goodness of the earth. It is not a solid stone slab. Metaphorically, agape love is like this rich and rugged terrain. The soil of agape is yielding enough to produce growth, uncompromising enough to demand depth, and rich enough to evoke quality in all that grows from it.

Without the rich, rocky soil of agape love, the other Fruit of the Spirit could not grow nor produce a harvest. As this hardy topography yields its fruit, each one evokes the essence of its source. Agape love is evident in every Fruit of the Spirit, each one yielding an eternally fragrant bouquet.

Love never fails; but if there are gifts of prophecy, they will be done away; if there are tongues, they will cease; if there is knowledge, it will be done away (1 Corinthians 13:8).

We would do well, then, to cultivate agape rich soil in our spiritual lives.

Loving Intolerance

In order to nurture the Fruit of the Spirit, certain conditions must not be tolerated just as vehemently as good soil is cultivated. For contrary to what is believed in our postmodern culture, intolerance is a facet of love.

Intolerance an aspect of love? What an unconventional notion, you may think. But consider this. Would you stand idly by and watch your closest friend willfully inflict harm on themselves? Would you remain passive at the sight of anyone abusing a child? Who among us is content to see those we love self-destruct through the addictions of alcohol, drugs, stress, or depression?

Right and wrong exist. Good and evil are resident in the world around us. Truth and falsehood are realities. The postmodern mantra *It's all good!* is a lie straight from the pit of Hell. Such a belief devastates the lives of those embracing it.

Sometimes the destruction is visible, as when weeds grow up in the vineyard to choke out the vine. At other times, spiritual devastation remains hidden beneath the surface like root rot or other subterranean blights. In both instances, we must be lovingly intolerant of such destruction by showing the agape love of Christ in ways that eradicate the disease of sin and its consequent death.

If a vineyard is afflicted with phylloxera, mold, or any number of destructive organisms, every effort is made to destroy the threat. The grower must be uncompromisingly intolerant of such devastating pests, knowing that left alone they could completely destroy the harvest. Similarly, behaviors that threaten agape love and all Fruit of the Spirit must not be tolerated in our lives or in those of others.

Behaving selfishly, being arrogant or boastful, acting rudely or behaving jealously are all counterproductive to spiritual fruit. However, in modern society, these traits are often touted as the very qualities that enable a person to get ahead in life.

As followers of Jesus Christ, will we tolerate these deleterious behaviors? Will we reason that such behavior might actually benefit those around us? Can we claim with any sense of reason that we are preferring one another and not putting ourselves first by behaving in these ways? In truth, we cannot defend any of these caustic behaviors because they are contrary to the nature of God.

Without Hypocrisy

A few years back, WWJD?—*What would Jesus do?*— was a popular slogan. Well, what would he do? How would he love those we consider unlovable? How should we? How would he love those we consider deserving of love? How should we love them? By considering his unchangeable nature, we can see clearly what our behavior ought to be.

Unfortunately, *WWJD?* was a passing fad for far too many. That should not be the case for those who truly follow Christ. If we, as his disciples, wish to exhibit the Fruit of his Spirit, we must first ground ourselves in the soil of agape love. We must love our enemies and pray for them, love our neighbors as ourselves, and love God above all else.

But I say to you, love your enemies and pray for those who persecute you (Matthew 5:44).

Pure agape love affirms the very nature of God. It is love without selfish motive. It is love that refuses to tolerate evil in the lives of others as well as in our own lives. Agape love does not compromise in its devotion to all that is good, for all that is good comes from our loving, Heavenly Father.

Every good thing given and every perfect gift is from above, coming down from the Father of lights, with whom there is no variation or shifting shadow (James 1:17).

Therefore, let us make Jesus, the embodiment of agape love, both our source and our goal as the Scripture says, "For from Him and through Him and to Him are all things" (Romans 11:36). If we fail to remain grounded in agape love, we remain incapable of producing any Fruit of the Spirit. Instead, earnestly heed the admonishment of the Apostle Paul who so eloquently sums up both the affirming and intolerant nature of the fruit of love.

Let love be without hypocrisy. Abhor what is evil; cling to what is good. Be devoted to one another in brotherly love; give preference to one another in honor . . . Do not be overcome by evil, but overcome evil with good (Romans 12:9-10, 21).

What have you harvested lately?

1. How unconditional is my love for God? For others?

2. Who do I struggle to love and why?

3. What can I do to increase my harvest of agape love?

4. What have I harvested lately?

A Symbiotic Crop

The Fruit of Joy

But the Fruit of the Spirit is love, joy, peace, patience, kindness, goodness, faithfulness, gentleness, self-control; against such things there is no law (Galatians 5:22-23).

You have put more joy in my heart than they have when their grain and wine abound (Psalm 4:7 ESV).

Joy Out of Season

Oh, to dwell in the joy of the Lord. Knowing that "the love of God has been poured out within our hearts through the Holy Spirit who was given to us" (Romans 5:5), we, of all people, have the most reason to rejoice. Likewise, knowing that we have been saved by grace given freely from the Father, nothing should prevent us from overflowing with joy.

> *For by grace you have been saved through faith; and that not of yourselves, it is the gift of God; not as a result of works, so that no one may boast* (Ephesians 2:89).

The Apostle Paul, who referred to himself as a wretched sinner, fully understood the symbiotic relationship between God's saving grace and this joy. In fact, it was precisely because of God's grace that Paul could rejoice in the hope of eternity with God rather than an eternity of eternal separation from his Creator. Paul's joy, and ours, stems naturally from standing rooted in God's grace.

> Through him we have also obtained access by faith into this grace in which we stand, and we rejoice in hope of the glory of God (Romans 5:2).

Yet, is it realistic to expect a person to exhibit joy in all of life's circumstances? Can you remain joyful in the face of adversity, in times of abject need, or in moments of agonizing sorrow? Is the grace of God sufficient in all of these situations? Well, yes his grace is sufficient, and especially so when our ability is not.

> *And He has said to me, "My grace is sufficient for you, for power is perfected in weakness." Most gladly, therefore, I will rather boast about my weaknesses, so that the power of Christ may dwell in me* (2 Corinthians 12:9).

Paul seems to have anticipated this concern about exhibiting ever-present joy when he wrote in verse 24 of Galatians 5, "Now those who belong to Christ Jesus have crucified the flesh with its passions and desires." He reminds us that once we belong to Christ, we have by choice died to our personal selfish desires. We yield our old nature over to death just as Christ yielded Himself to death by crucifixion.

Earlier in Galatians, Paul asserts that since he is crucified with Christ, the life he now lives is by faith and his righteousness is the result of God's grace.

I have been crucified with Christ; and it is no longer I who live, but Christ lives in me; and the life which I now live in the flesh I live by faith in the Son of God, who loved me and gave Himself up for me. I do not nullify the grace of God, for if righteousness comes through the Law, then Christ died needlessly (Galatians 2:20-21).

If this isn't a cause for rejoicing, I'm not sure what is.

But what does dying to selfish desire have to do with bearing the fruit of joy? For one thing, Paul is not asserting that exhibiting joy means Christians never experience sorrow or sadness. By no means.

Instead, he is encouraging us that when difficult seasons of life occur, we must choose to master our emotions through God's grace, which enables us to remain undaunted in producing the fruit of joy. Joy, especially out of season when it is least expected, is a source of blessing, for oneself as well as others.

A Paradoxical Fruit

To gain insight into this seeming contradiction of joy in difficult times, consider Jesus on his way to Jerusalem for his final Passover with the disciples, as depicted in Mark's

Gospel. The story begins with Jesus' triumphal entry into Jerusalem:

> *As they approached Jerusalem, at Bethphage and Bethany, near the Mount of Olives, He sent two of His disciples, and said to them, "Go into the village opposite you, and immediately as you enter it, you will find a colt tied there,"*
>
> *They brought the colt to Jesus and put their coats on it; and He sat on it. And many spread their coats in the road, and others spread leafy branches which they had cut from the fields. Those who went in front and those who followed were shouting: "Hosanna! Blessed is He who comes in the name of the LORD;"*
> (Mark 11:1-2a, 7-9).

Can you imagine the excitement and victory the disciples were experiencing on their return to Bethany that evening? The Lord's deliberate survey of the Temple must have appeared to them as reconnaissance for what he planned to do on the morrow.

The disciples surely thought, *This is it!* This had to be the eve of Jesus setting up his messianic throne in Jerusalem, and they were to be his inner circle. Oh, the visions of power, authority, prestige and celebrity they must have anticipated.

In the cool of the next morning's dawn, they set out for the day brimming with expectation at what was about to transpire. They'd probably slept little, if any, as their minds raced through all of the possible scenarios about to unfold. Given the exuberant welcome by the throngs in Jerusalem's streets, they were certain Jesus was ready to make his move.

First among his planned expulsions of the day would no doubt be the Sanhedrin and the High Priest, the core of the corruption permeating Israel. Would Jesus shame them into contrition? Would he remove them bodily from the Temple

Mount? Or would he simply speak a word and curse them into oblivion? Anything seemed possible.

Perhaps the Twelve were too wrapped up in their own thoughts to notice that Jesus was unusually quiet. Regardless, they cavorted like yeshiva boys as they walked the few miles between Bethany and Jerusalem. No one seemed to remember that they'd not taken time to eat breakfast on that clear and fragrant springtime morning. Drawing nearer to the city, Jesus spied a towering fig tree, spreading its glossy green leaves like a canopy.

On the next day, when they had left Bethany, He became hungry. Seeing at a distance a fig tree in leaf, He went to see if perhaps He would find anything on it (Mark 11:12-13a).

Figs. How Jesus enjoyed figs. They grew all around his base of operation in the northern Galil. It was under a fig tree such as this that Jesus first saw Nathanael, a man in whom he said there was no guile (John 1:47). Jesus had many fond memories of reclining in the canopied shade of such trees, munching their fruit.

Like the days that lay before Jesus and his band of talmidim (Hebrew for disciples), figs are a paradoxical fruit. The sweet and satisfying fruit itself is wrapped in a course, unyielding skin. Such irony was surely not lost on Jesus as he approached the fig tree on his morning ascent into Jerusalem. Brimming with anticipation, Jesus' mouth began to water.

The irony of the morning continued when Peter uttered a groan of dissatisfaction at Jesus' eagerness to pick the tree's fruit for his breakfast. Peter may have exclaimed derisively, *Figs*?! He'd eaten them every day of his life growing up in Capernaum. How he'd grown tired of them. Now he only ate them to be polite when a gracious hostess served them for a meal. But to eat them now on such a day brimming with expectations, well, he'd rather go without. Peter, like the other eleven, was eager to get to Jerusalem without delay to see the Kingdom ushered in.

So, amidst these reflections and taunts aimed at Peter whom all knew to detest the fruit, Jesus sprinted up the hill to the tree. "Last one up the hill's a rotten fig!" someone called in boyish challenge. Walking toward the tree in full expectation of a tangy morning meal, Jesus reached toward the branches.

But the tree was barren of fruit. Jesus' disappointment was palpable. In fact, he seemed right down angry. In a wrathful tone that the Twelve thought would be suitable for castigating Caiaphas, the Lord exclaimed, "May no one ever eat fruit from you again!" And his disciples were listening (Mark 11:14).

Such disdain for a fruitless tree. What can we learn of joy from this vignette?

Faithful Over Little, Faithful Over Much

Before we come to that, however, it must be pointed out that in Mark's Gospel, the writer notes that it was not the season for figs; "and when He came to it, He found nothing but leaves, for it was not the season for figs" (Mark 11:13). This makes sense, of course, since it was springtime—and not autumn when fruit crops are harvested.

Yet Jesus expected to find figs on the tree. What a quandary this presents, until we learn that fig trees produce two crops each year. In the spring, the time when Jesus was going to Passover, the fig tree should have already produced what is called the breba crop. This is a small crop of edible, if less than succulent figs that begin to emerge before the tree's branches are fully ensconced with leaves.

Once the tree is in the full foliage of late springtime, it is completely reasonable to anticipate a crop of tiny but edible buds growing from beneath the waxy leaves. This is what

Jesus expected to find. The breba crop is the promise of a far more fulfilling crop to be harvested later in the fall.

Perhaps Jesus was thinking of his talmidim as he spied the barren fig tree. How he desired that they would be faithful to produce even a small crop of joy in the coming days in order to fully rejoice once his victory over sin and death became evident.

Jesus wasn't being unreasonable in his expectation to find fruit on the tree even though it wasn't the season for the full harvest. But since the tree wasn't producing even the out-of-season crop, he cursed it, knowing that it was incapable of bearing a fall harvest. It would never produce anything ever again. And it didn't.

As they were passing by [the following] morning, they saw the fig tree withered from the roots up (Mark 11:20).

Do you see how this relates to our responsibility to produce the fruit of joy? Like the fig tree, we are to bear joy both in and out of season. Regardless of how large the crop, there is an expectation that it should be ever present in our lives and that it should refresh the lives of those we encounter.

How well are you producing joy in all that you do? Does your joy bless others as well as yourself? Does your joy in difficult times demonstrate the assurance of joy in times of celebration?

This expectation to be productive regardless of the season or the size of the harvest is also reminiscent of the parable of the talents. Consider the story as found in the Gospel of Matthew:

For it is just like a man about to go on a journey, who called his own slaves and entrusted his possessions to them. To one he gave five talents, to another, two, and to another, one, each according to his own ability; and he went on his journey. . .

Now after a long time the master of those slaves came and settled accounts with them. The one who had received the five talents came up and brought five more talents . . . His master said to him, "Well done, good and faithful slave. . .

Also the one who had received the two talents came up and said, "Master, you entrusted two talents to me. See, I have gained two more talents." His master said to him, "Well done, good and faithful slave. . .

And the one also who had received the one talent came up and said, "Master, I knew you to be a hard man . . . I was afraid, and went away and hid your talent in the ground. See, you have what is yours."

But his master answered and said to him, "You wicked, lazy slave . . . Therefore take away the talent from him, and give it to the one who has the ten talents."

For to everyone who has, more shall be given, and he will have an abundance; but from the one who does not have, even what he does have shall be taken away. Throw out the worthless slave into the outer darkness; in that place there will be weeping and gnashing of teeth (Matthew 25:14-30).

When the master of the story returns and discovers that some servants have been faithful to produce a profit for him, he blesses them. But the unfaithful servant, who didn't even produce a meager gain from putting his master's money on interest, this servant is cursed. And not only is he cursed, what he has is taken from him and given to another. Verse 29 sums up the moral of the story:

For to everyone who has, more shall be given, and he will have an abundance; but from the one who does not have, even what he does have shall be taken away.

The parallels between the cursed fig tree and the negligent servant should be quite obvious. Both were cursed and prevented from ever propagating a full harvest because each failed to first produce a small harvest.

Grace for Joy

Our responsibility to produce joy is much the same. Like the figs, joy must be produced in season and out of season. Like the talents, we must bear joy regardless of whether we reap a bumper crop or a simple handful. In our lives it matters not if conditions are favorable or unfavorable for sustaining a crop of joy. Either way, the fruit of joy must still be evident in our lives.

Written in one of my Bibles is this quote: "Christian joy is independent of outward circumstances." I've lost track of who said this, but over the years it has encouraged me not to indulge in self-pity, depression, or an attitude of defeat. Happiness may depend on circumstances, but the joy of the Lord does not.

Paul himself was well versed at persisting in a joyful disposition regardless of circumstances. In Philippians he reminds us to rejoice in the Lord at all times:

Rejoice in the Lord always; again I will say, rejoice!
(Philippians 4:4).

Later in the chapter Paul expounds further on the nature of his rejoicing, saying that he has learned to rejoice in every situation, be it good or bad:

But I rejoiced in the Lord greatly, that now at last you have revived your concern for me; indeed, you were concerned before, but you lacked opportunity. Not that I speak from want, for I have learned to be content in whatever circumstances I am.

I know how to get along with humble means, and I also know how to live in prosperity; in any and every circumstance I have learned the secret of being filled and going hungry, both of having abundance and suffering need. I can do all things through Him who strengthens me (Philippians 4:10-13).

In learning to be content regardless of what was happening around him, Paul was able to rejoice continually. Given the list of his personal sufferings described in 2 Corinthians, Paul has proven himself the quintessential model of joyfulness no matter what.

Are they servants of Christ?—I speak as if insane—I more so; in far more labors, in far more imprisonments, beaten times without number, often in danger of death.

Five times I received from the Jews thirty-nine lashes. Three times I was beaten with rods, once I was stoned, three times I was shipwrecked, a night and a day I have spent in the deep. I have been on frequent journeys, in dangers from rivers, dangers from robbers, dangers from my countrymen, dangers from the Gentiles, dangers in the city, dangers in the wilderness, dangers on the sea, dangers among false brethren; I have been in labor and hardship, through many sleepless nights, in hunger and thirst, often without food, in cold and exposure (2 Corinthians 11:23-27).

Given this litany of trials, can't you hear Paul's Amen! to Peter's words penned in this his first epistle?

Beloved, do not be surprised at the fiery ordeal among you, which comes upon you for your testing, as though some strange thing were happening to you; but to the degree that you share the sufferings of Christ, keep on rejoicing, so that also at the revelation of His glory you may rejoice with exultation (1 Peter 4:12-13).

Perhaps it is not surprising that Peter and Paul could maintain joy in the middle of adversity. They were Apostles after all. But what about us? If we are to have joy regardless of circumstance, where do we find the strength? What is the source of this overriding joy?

I believe that what truly enables the Believer to live in a pervasive state of joy is the unmerited grace of God. "For by grace you have been saved through faith; and that not of yourselves, it is the gift of God" (Ephesians 2:8). The Greek word for grace is *charis* (χάρισ) which is related to the Greek word for joy, *chara* (χαρά).

We have been saved by the charis of God, his free and unearned favor. This should provide sufficient impetus for us to remain in a constant state of chara, joy. And truly his grace is sufficient to provide our salvation, sustain our joy, and supply all we need.

As I reflect on the fruit of joy, the refrain of an old worship chorus comes to mind. "He gives joy unspeakable and full of glory." May you be filled with this unspeakable joy as you rest in the unmerited grace of God and produce the fruit of joy in every season of your life.

For You make him most blessed forever; You make him joyful with gladness in Your presence (Psalm 21:6).

What have you harvested lately?

1. When is it easy for me to be joyful? When do I find it difficult?

2. Who might I bless by being more joyful in my life?

3. What can I do to increase my harvest of joy?

4. What have I harvested lately?

An Inexplicable Crop
The Fruit of Peace

But the Fruit of the Spirit is love, joy, peace, patience, kindness, goodness, faithfulness, gentleness, self-control; against such things there is no law (Galatians 5:22-23).

Peace I leave with you; My peace I give to you; not as the world gives do I give to you. Do not let your heart be troubled, nor let it be fearful (John 14:27).

Headline News

Jesus spoke these words to his disciples shortly before the crucifixion. The comment must have puzzled the Twelve. Why should they be concerned about troubles and fears? Wasn't Jesus about to set up the Kingdom of Heaven on Earth? It was only later that these words must have come back to them with a sobering depth of meaning.

In the midst of the Lord's trial, conviction and subsequent death, they must have been terrified, anticipating that they were next to hang on the crosses lining the road into Jerusalem. During the three days the Lord lay in the tomb, did the Twelve recall his encouragement to be at peace? Before he rose from the dead, were they able to grasp what manner of peace he'd given them? It must have been unimaginable to cling to peace when their world was falling apart all around them.

Today, just as it was in first-century Israel, our world is in turmoil. Almost daily we read headlines such as these.

Nearly 3000 Die in Terrorist Attacks on September 11

Devastating Hurricanes Leave Thousands Homeless

Suicide Bombers Target Israeli Bus Station

Bridge Collapse Kills 13, Dozens Injured

Miners Trapped, Feared Dead and Unrecoverable

8.0 Earthquake Devastates Peru

Toys Pose Lead Poisoning Danger to Children

Fires Consume Thousands of Acres in Western US States

8.0 Earthquake Ravishes China

Sub-Prime Lending Crashes Global Markets

Hearing of such news whether online, in print, or broadcast on any of the many 24/7 cable news networks can leave us feeling many things. Like the disciples witnessing Jesus' death, we may feel fearful, confused, anxious, angry or abandoned. But remaining peaceful is not an obvious response.

In today's global community, we are no longer only aware of what is happening in our own back yard, so to speak. Now we see on live television what is occurring around the world. Famines here. Tsunamis there. Wars and conflicts on nearly every continent. And national economies are now so closely linked that a major change in one ripples through the rest.

But certainly it's not all bleak out there. There are headlines that proffer hope:

Law and Justice Win in Poland

Czech Average Wage on the Rise

Families Open Homes to Hurricane Evacuees

Heroic Helicopter Rescue of Flood Victims

Philanthropist Donates $70 Million to Colleges

Selfless Acts of Kindness Amongst Bridge Collapse Victims

Young Teachers Commit to Denver's Toughest Schools

Yet current events, good or bad, remain unable to bring the internal, abiding sense of peace and contentment that people so desire. The world may offer peace, but it is never truly lasting peace.

So how are we as Christians to remain peaceful in spite of circumstances? If we stay peaceful, won't we be viewed as unsympathetic or unconcerned for the welfare of others who seem more directly impacted by turmoil? Won't we seem naïve or be viewed as a *Pollyanna*? Perhaps, or perhaps not. Besides, what our Lord expects of us far outweighs what people think.

Something Inexplicable

Let's consider phrase by phrase what we can learn about this peace given to us by Jesus. Re-read John 14:27 and notice all that you observe about peace:

> *Peace I leave with you; My peace I give to you; not as the world gives do I give to you. Do not let your heart be troubled, nor let it be fearful* (John 14:27).

The first thing we observe is that Jesus left peace with us and gave it to us. In fact, he states twice that he has given us this peace. The Greek word for "leave" is *afiami* (ἀφίημι), which carries the legal connotation of things left to someone in a last will and testament. In effect, Jesus is saying that upon his death, the disciples are written into his will to receive his peace.

I imagine they may have thought Jesus was being rather dramatic, and maybe even just a bit chintzy. Remember they were expecting Jesus to be crowned King very soon, not to be crucified and die.

To clarify that this peace wasn't something they'd receive one day far into the future, Jesus emphasizes that he is giving them this peace right then by saying twice in the present tense "I give to you" (*didomi umin*, δίδωμι ὑμῖν). The disciples, like ourselves, are to receive the peace our Lord has given to us right now in every circumstance.

Let's next consider the nature of the peace Jesus has given us. This isn't just any old garden-variety sort of peace. This is the very peace of the Lord himself. "My peace I give to you." In Ephesians, Paul tells us that Jesus himself "is our peace" (Ephesians 2:14), and that he has "preached peace to [us] who were far away, and peace to those who were near" (Ephesians 2:17).

So the peace we've been given is Christ himself and it is given not only for the disciples, those who were near, but to those of us who would receive Christ far in the future. That means us!

In the event that Jesus has still not gotten through to the disciples, or to us for that matter, concerning the significance of this peace, he goes on to assure us that what we've been given is "not as the world gives." The peace of Jesus isn't a transient feeling dependent on everything going well in our lives. That's the peace of the world. Our peace, the peace of the Holy Spirit, is constant, eternal, and independent of what we see, feel, or experience. This is hybrid spiritual fruit that should comprise an abundant portion of our spiritual harvest.

Finally, Jesus clarifies the effect of his peace in our lives. With this gift of the Lord's peace, we need not be troubled in our hearts, nor should we be fearful. With Jesus' abiding peace we have no need to be disturbed, unsettled, troubled, frightened, nor should we be timid or cowardly.

If his peace prevents us from behaving in these ways, how then should we behave? We should do just the opposite. We should be unconcerned, at ease, calm, unafraid, as well as bold and courageous.

In your life, are you producing the peace of Jesus Christ? Is your peace independent of what occurs around you? Are you impacting the lives of others through your calm and courageous demeanor? Take heart that you can be bold and unafraid through Christ as you sow and reap your harvest of peace. It is this supernatural peace that Paul expects us to bear as a Fruit of the Spirit in our daily lives.

When Jesus told the disciples that he was leaving his peace with them, he left them an inexplicable peace that would carry them through the most daunting of circumstances. They may not have understood the significance of this peace at the moment, but they would eventually. How could they begin to imagine what it would be like to receive the absolute peace of God? Why don't you take time right now to give thanks for this inexplicable gift that has been given to you.

So Far as It Depends on You

As we learn to walk in peace and pursue peace, we see its effect not only in our own lives but also in the lives of those around us. The writer of Hebrews tells us that as we endeavor to live peacefully with other people, we are also pursuing their sanctification:

Pursue peace with all men, and the sanctification without which no one will see the Lord (Hebrews 12:14).

James furthers this notion that salvation in the lives of those we touch is a byproduct of walking in peace. In effect, he says that the seed of salvation that is deposited peacefully into the lives of others will take root and bear the fruit of salvation which is righteousness.

And the seed whose fruit is righteousness is sown in peace by those who make peace (James 3:18).

This means that when sharing the Gospel, the Good News of Jesus Christ, we are to do so in a peaceful, non-contentious manner. There is no need to become combative; in fact, if we become combative in presenting the Gospel we are destroying the seed of salvation before it ever has a chance to take root. Whether sharing the Gospel, discussing the stock market, reviewing world events, or discussing Scripture, we would do well to remain peaceful which brings with it a confident assurance that remains unruffled by dissenting opinions.

Peter further encourages us toward living a life of peace in our actions, attitudes and affirmations. Quoting from Psalm 34, Peter has this to say:

To sum up, all of you be harmonious, sympathetic, brotherly, kindhearted, and humble in spirit; not returning evil for evil or insult for insult, but giving a blessing instead; for you were called for the very purpose that you might inherit a blessing. For, "The one who desires life, to love and see good days, must keep his tongue from evil and his lips from speaking deceit. He must turn away from evil and do good; he must seek peace and pursue it" (1 Peter 8:11).

Pursuing peace means that we live harmoniously, sympathetically, walking in brotherly love, kindness and humility. We are not to retaliate but to speak blessings. Neither are we to lie or speak abusive words. As we avoid such evil behavior and pursue peace, we are assured of living a blessed life, abounding with love, and good days. Now that's what I call a bountiful harvest.

When this peace that surpasses our understanding takes root and grows in our hearts, it is only natural for us to share it with those around us, spreading its seeds into their hearts. These seeds of peace will bear the further fruit of sanctification and righteousness.

Is it any wonder, then, that Jesus pronounced a special blessing on those who pursue and make peace? In his Sermon on the Mount, Jesus said that peacemakers are blessed and will be called the sons of God (Matthew 5:9). Oh, to hear such a blessing.

Toward that end, Paul encourages us that whenever possible, "so far as it depends on you, be at peace with all men" (Romans 12:18).

What prevents you from living in peace, from spreading it into the lives of others? Do you allow the concerns of the world, the trials in your life, the words of other people to steal away your peace? Do you attempt to handle the difficulties of your life all on your own? If you do, your peace will begin to diminish.

This is exactly what the enemy, Satan, wants; he wants the weeds of worry and concern and defeat to choke out your harvest of peace. But when you cast all your cares on Christ, the weeds of anxiety are destroyed and you are empowered to walk in the confidence of God's peace.

Therefore humble yourselves under the mighty hand of God, that He may exalt you at the proper time, casting all your anxiety on Him, because He cares for you.

Be of sober spirit, be on the alert. Your adversary, the devil, prowls around like a roaring lion, seeking someone to devour (1 Peter 5:6-8).

As you receive Christ's peace and relinquish your anxieties and concerns to him, you will harvest a bumper crop of peace that blesses both you and everyone else who is touched by your peace. As you persevere toward this goal, be encouraged with these words from Paul written to the church at Philippi;

Be anxious for nothing, but in everything by prayer and supplication with thanksgiving let your requests be made known to God. And the peace of God, which surpasses all comprehension, will guard your hearts and your minds in Christ Jesus (Philippians 4:6-7).

What have you harvested lately?

1. What weeds of concern and worry have I allowed to choke out my peace?

2. Whose life have I brought peace to?

3. How can I pursue more of Jesus' hybrid peace in my life?

4. What have I harvested lately?

An Unconventional Crop
The Fruit of Patience

But the Fruit of the Spirit is love, joy, peace, patience, kindness, goodness, faithfulness, gentleness, self-control; against such things there is no law (Galatians 5:22-23).

The end of a matter is better than its beginning; patience of spirit is better than haughtiness of spirit (Proverbs 7:8).

The Appointed Time

St. Augustine called patience the companion of wisdom. It has also been called the greatest of all virtues. Aristotle noted that while patience may be in itself bitter, its fruit is indeed sweet. Peter Marshall, pastor and former U.S. Senate Chaplain, offered this prayer concerning patience: "Teach us, O Lord, the disciplines of patience, for to wait is often harder than to work." Perhaps it is not without significance that the fruit of patience follows after love, joy and peace. For without the manifestation of these in our lives, I fear it would be impossible to exhibit the fruit of patience.

Jesus knew a great deal about patience. Being both fully God and fully man, he waited patiently from the fall of Adam and Eve in the Garden until his time came to redeem mankind from sin.

> *In the beginning was the Word, and the Word was with God, and the Word was God. He was in the beginning with God. . . .*
>
> *But as many as received Him, to them He gave the right to become children of God, even to those who believe in His name, who were born, not of blood nor of the will of the flesh nor of the will of man, but of God* (John 1:1-3, 12-13).
>
> *For while we were still helpless, at the right time Christ died for the ungodly* (Romans 5:6).

Even now he is patiently waiting for the appointed time of his return when he will judge the living and the dead and establish his kingdom.

> *Jesus said to him, "You have said it yourself; nevertheless I tell you, hereafter you will see the Son of Man sitting at the right hand of Power, and coming on the clouds of heaven"* (Matthew 26:64).

*For the Son of Man is going to come in the glory of
His Father with His angels, and will then repay
every man according to his deeds* (Matthew 16:27).

While relating to this level of divine patience is beyond
us, we can relate to examples of Jesus' patience when he
resided in our world as the son of a carpenter from Nazareth.

Agrarian Life

Located in the southern region of Galilee, Nazareth is
situated about midway between the Mediterranean Sea and
the Jordan River. Surrounded by limestone hills, it lay at the
intersection of numerous trade routes.

Merchants traveled through Nazareth to and from all
directions. From the seacoast came imported textiles, iron
ore, and exotic delicacies imported from Rome's vast
empire. Olives and olive oil were brought from Samaria,
along with honey and wheat from the fields surrounding Beit
Shean. Joseph and his son must have waited anxiously to
receive shipments of cedar from Lebanon's forests or dark
walnut planks from the northern Galil, which they crafted
into beams and lintels to build many a home for the Nazareth
community.

Nazareth must have been bustling with activity. Even so,
the pace of life was much slower than today, and it kept time
to the seasons of the fields. Between the early rains of
autumn and the frigid snows of winter, the fields were
ploughed and sown in anticipation of grain harvests in the
spring. With the first blooms of the almond tree in the chilly
air of Shebat (late January to February), winter shed its
leaden shroud. Springtime truly emerged with the latter rains
and the harvests of barley and flax.

During the intervening months, the vineyards, fields, and
orchards of the Galil were a riot of colors, textures, scents
and sounds as crops were tended and gathered into the
storehouses or exported to other regions of the Land of

Promise. Then as the cooling early rains of autumn returned, the annual cycle of sowing and reaping began again.

This agrarian pace of life so permeated the lives of all who lived in the land during the time of Christ that— whether living in city, town, or farm—everyone was attuned to seed time and harvest. Such a life taught patience out of necessity.

If it wasn't the season for dates, one had to wait. If there were no pomegranates left in the larder, one had to wait for the next harvest. Once the grapes ran out, raisins would have to do. Living a lifestyle of such patience provided vivid illustrations that taught patience in other, more significant aspects of life.

> *Therefore be patient, brethren, until the coming of the Lord. The farmer waits for the precious produce of the soil, being patient about it, until it gets the early and late rains. You too be patient; strengthen your hearts, for the coming of the Lord is near* (James 5:7-8).

Lessons from the Heartland

Like the populace of first-century Israel, Iowa farmers raising their crops in the heartland of America's Corn Belt know a great deal about patience. Every year, they are out early in spring, preparing their fields for planting. They disc and plough the ebony-colored soil to prepare it. The fields are boisterous with activity soon after the last drifts of snow have mostly melted away.

Once the fields are prepared and the corn is planted, the pace of activity slows down a bit. The wait has begun for the first heads of young seedlings to break through the earth, reaching toward brilliant blue skies.

Depending on the weather and soil conditions, in a couple of weeks a faint hint of green begins to appear and define the carefully cultivated rows. Some fields are ribboned with curving rows that follow the contours of nearby rivers or streambeds. Others emerge like a field of ancient MacDonald tartan with neat rows of bright green seedlings crosscut by swaths of coal-black soil.

But the time for biting into juicy ears of sweet corn is well down the road. Harvest won't come for another four to five months. Farmers understand patience.

Modern society is far less agrarian than it was even in recent generations. Unless you grew up on a farm or are one of the fortunate few still harvesting the family homestead, you've more than likely become accustom to a faster, on-demand pace of life. Patience is an unconventional crop to produce in our modern world.

Today we're eagerly dependent on microwaves, fast food, on-demand movies, and every other type of instant gratification imaginable. We are continually barraged by get-rich-quick schemes, 48-hour weight-loss concoctions, instant music and movie downloads, and immediate approval to acquire mountains of debt.

So where's the need for patience?

For one thing, Proverbs 13:11 warns that, "Wealth gained hastily will dwindle, but whoever gathers little by little will increase it" (ESV). Like the kernels of corn planted in the farmer's field, patience yields a bountiful crop when properly and deliberately tended. Just as succulent roasting ears cannot be harvested over night, neither can the benefits of patience be gleaned on demand.

Think about the following Scripture and reflect on the benefits gained by employing patience, endurance, long suffering, and perseverance:

Consider it all joy, my brethren, when you encounter various trials, knowing that the testing of your faith produces endurance. And let endurance have its perfect result, so that you may be perfect and complete, lacking in nothing (James 1:2-4).

According to James, patient endurance results in our perfection, completion, and the full supply of all we need.

For you have need of endurance, so that when you have done the will of God, you may receive what was promised (Hebrews 10:36).

The writer of Hebrews tells us that patient endurance enables us to do God's will and to then receive his promises.

For this finds favor, if for the sake of conscience toward God a person bears up under sorrows when suffering unjustly. For what credit is there if, when you sin and are harshly treated, you endure it with patience? But if when you do what is right and suffer for it you patiently endure it, this finds favor with God (1 Peter 2:19-20).

What blessings abound in finding the favor of God through the practice of patience!

And not only this, but we also exult in our tribulations, knowing that tribulation brings about perseverance; and perseverance, proven character; and proven character, hope; and hope does not disappoint, because the love of God has been poured out within our hearts through the Holy Spirit who was given to us (Romans 5:3-5).

Perseverance brings about character, which leads to hope, which eradicates disappointment, and culminates with the love of God filling us through the Holy Spirit. If these blessings don't get us motivated to be patient, I don't know if anything will.

Patience for the Promise

There is a balance here, of course. Solomon reminds us in Ecclesiastes 3:1 that there "is an appointed time for everything. And there is a time for every event under heaven." He speaks of a time to plant and to harvest, to build up and to tear down, to embrace and to refrain, to speak and to be silent.

How then will we know when to wait patiently and when to take action? To know this, we must continually seek the Lord in prayer and in his Word. We must be certain not to usurp his authority by acting on our own outside of faith in him.

James encourages us in chapter 4 verse 17 that "to one who knows the right thing to do and does not do it, to him it is sin." We must be patient to act when and how God instructs us to instead of merely acting on our own.

Abraham and Sarah learned this lesson the hard way, and as a consequence, the effects of their actions are still evident in our world today. Rather than wait patiently for God to fulfill his promise of a son in spite of what seemed to be insurmountable obstacles, Sarah and Abraham took matters into their own hands. They rationalized that since Sarah was long past the age of bearing children, the logical thing would be for Abraham to father a child by a surrogate.

So they reasoned through God's promise and relied on their own methods to see it fulfilled. Ishmael was the son born through their manipulation. Only later was Isaac, the son of promise, born through Sarah. To this day, Ishmael's descendents live in defiance of the Sons of Promise, just as Scripture foretold.

The angel of the LORD said to [Hagar] further, "Behold, you are with child, And you will bear a son; And you shall call his name Ishmael, Because the LORD has given heed to your affliction. He will be a wild donkey of a man, His hand will be against everyone, And everyone's hand will be against him; And he will live to the east of all his brothers" (Genesis 16:11-12).

These are the sons of Ishmael and these are their names, by their villages, and by their camps; twelve princes according to their tribes. These are the years of the life of Ishmael, one hundred and thirty-seven years; and he breathed his last and died, and was gathered to his people. They settled from Havilah to Shur which is east of Egypt as one goes toward Assyria; [Ishmael] settled in defiance of all his relatives (Genesis 25:16-18).

What a different world we would live in today if Abraham and Sarah had only waited patiently for the promise, instead of settling for their own manipulative compromise.

So the question comes to each of us. If we rely on our own strength, our own intellect or our own craftiness to bring about God's will, are we patiently waiting for him to fulfill his promise? If the farmer becomes impatient with the crop and uncovers the seed in an effort to assist it in breaking through the soil, the crop will wither and die.

Like the farmer, we must wait patiently and have faith that even though the process cannot be seen, the promise of harvest is being fulfilled. Abraham and Sarah certainly had to act in order to conceive Isaac. But even then, they could not see what God was bringing forth. Their obedience to both act and wait patiently were based on faith; "the assurance of things hoped for, the conviction of things not seen" (Hebrews 11:1). In contrast, their impatience and manipulation were based on doubt.

Only when we wait patiently on the Lord will we receive his promise. And his promise is full of eternal bounty. Patience brings about our perfection, completion, and provision; it brings God's favor; it develops our character and gives us hope. The choice then is ours. We can choose Ishmael or Isaac, the manipulation or the promise.

The words of King David encourage us to develop this unconventional crop called patience. Here is a man who truly knew what it meant to wait patiently for God. Even after spending years as a fugitive on the run from his predecessor, King Saul, David continued to wait patiently for the fulfillment of the Lord's promise to place him on Israel's throne.

I waited patiently for the LORD; and He inclined to me and heard my cry. He brought me up out of the pit of destruction, out of the miry clay, and He set my feet upon a rock making my footsteps firm. He put a new song in my mouth, a song of praise to our God; many will see and fear and will trust in the LORD. So let us wait with patience upon our Lord (Psalm 40:1-3).

May each of us enjoy a harvest of patience as we learn to wait with expectation, knowing that God will perform his will at his appointed time. Toward that end, Habakkuk offers us this encouragement:

For the vision is yet for the appointed time; it hastens toward the goal and it will not fail. Though it tarries, wait for it; for it will certainly come, it will not delay (Habakkuk 2:3).

What have you harvested lately?

1. How abundant is my harvest of patience?

2. Who am I impacting most when I behave impatiently? When I am patient?

3. What can I do to develop the fruit of patience in my daily life?

4. What have I harvested lately?

A Selfless Crop

The Fruit of Kindness

But the Fruit of the Spirit is love, joy, peace, patience, kindness, goodness, faithfulness, gentleness, self-control; against such things there is no law (Galatians 5:22-23).

Sow with a view to righteousness, reap in accordance with kindness; break up your fallow ground, for it is time to seek the LORD until He comes to rain righteousness on you (Hosea 10:12).

Seasons Greetings

Kindness is a character trait set aside by many during most of the year, only to be dusted off during the holiday seasons of Thanksgiving, Christmas and, Hanukkah. Then in a rush to be post marked before December 31st, people who have spoken few if any kind words for the preceding ten or eleven months race about sending dozens of warm and fuzzy greeting cards. Charitable contributions at kettle, cup, and tzedakah box likewise abound during the holidays.

Throughout the winter months, even those who are generally far less than kind rediscover hidden reserves of mercy and charity deep within themselves. Gifts flow freely; the poor are remembered; and the sad and hungry are provided for. But do such actions truly exhibit the fruit of kindness? Or does kindness perhaps involve much more than coins in the coffer?

The generous expressions of love, joy, peace and patience are clearly seen in true acts of kindness. Webster's dictionary describes such behavior as benevolent, good-natured, helpful, friendly, or cordial.

And truly, kindness is all these things. William Wordsworth echoed Scripture when he said that the best part of a man's life is "his little, nameless, unremembered acts of kindness and of love." And Nachman of Bratslav, a Hasidic rabbi who lived around the turn of the 19th century wrote, "Through charity and kindness a man attains to godliness."

It is interesting that the Greek word Paul uses for kindness in Galatians 5:22 is *chrastotas* (χρηστότησ), which can also be translated as goodness. Goodness, *agathosuna* (ἀγαθωσύνη), is, of course, the next spiritual fruit following kindness. Paul, as we would expect is being very deliberate in his vocabulary. For while both chrastotas and agathosuna can be translated the same, chrastotas (translated as kindness) expresses a sense of relationship while agathosuna (translated as goodness) describes a person's character.

In other words, chrastotas is goodness performed on behalf of another person. Thus kindness is distinguished from goodness as being an act of benevolence performed for the benefit of someone other than oneself. Goodness, on the other hand, describes the temperament of the person performing the kind act.

Another distinguishing characteristic of kindness is that the Greek chrastotas also pertains to truthfulness, respectability, and worthiness which are often used in conjunction with the performance of philanthropy. Given Paul's education in the Hebrew Scriptures, it is little wonder that he used this specific term to depict acts of kindness. For in the Old Testament, kindness is often paired with truth as well as with justice.

Do not let kindness and truth leave you; bind them around your neck, write them on the tablet of your heart (Proverbs 3:3).

Thus has the LORD of hosts said, "Dispense true justice and practice kindness and compassion each to his brother; and do not oppress the widow or the orphan, the stranger or the poor; and do not devise evil in your hearts against one another" (Zechariah 7:9-10).

He has told you, O man, what is good; and what does the LORD require of you but to do justice, to love kindness, and to walk humbly with your God? (Micah 6:8).

Kind, Just and True

To show another person kindness is to uphold justice and proclaim truth, to behave with respect for right and wrong, and to do so with honesty. To do otherwise would be a demonstration of injustice, falsehood, and cruelty—all of which are contrary to the genuine expression of kindness. Let's consider further the relationship between kindness, justice and truth.

God is a God of justice. We read of his justice in Isaiah:

Therefore the LORD longs to be gracious to you, and therefore He waits on high to have compassion on you. For the LORD is a God of justice; how blessed are all those who long for Him (Isaiah 30:18).

We also learn of the just and upright nature of our Lord God from the psalmist:

For the word of the LORD is upright, and all His work is done in faithfulness. He loves righteousness and justice; the earth is full of the lovingkindness of the LORD (Psalm 33:4-5).

If justice is a defining characteristic of God, then certainly injustice is completely opposed to his nature. This is indeed true because injustice is the height of unkindness and cruelty. Punishing the innocent, rewarding the evildoer, hoarding wealth, and refusing to offer compassion—these are all acts of injustice.

Consequently, extending compassion, provision, and justice are the acts of kindness that God demonstrates toward us and that he requires of us. Showing compassion and provision to the innocent, rewarding good and punishing evil, giving out of our abundance—all these can be described as equally just and kind. Kindness is a natural outflow of justice.

In addition to its alliance with justice, kindness also upholds truth, which is inextricably intertwined with justice. Truth will always result in justice, and justice cannot exist where there is no truth. And since kindness is a natural outflow of justice, the relationship between these three virtues is seen. Consider the following passage from the

Psalms that clearly depicts these virtues as being descriptive of the Lord God:

Righteousness and justice are the foundation of Your throne; Lovingkindness and truth go before You (Psalm 89:14).

If God's very throne is situated on righteousness and justice, shouldn't our lives be likewise grounded? And if lovingkindness and truth proceed before him, shouldn't we also walk in the same manner? Indeed our lives should reflect all aspects of God's nature. Consider Peter's words of admonition:

His divine power has granted to us everything pertaining to life and godliness, through the true knowledge of Him who called us by His own glory and excellence. For by these He has granted to us His precious and magnificent promises, so that by them you may become partakers of the divine nature, (2 Peter 1:3-4).

This relationship of truth, justice, and kindness is often depicted in Scripture by references to truthful and just scales. In Deuteronomy, we are instructed not to have differing weights by which we do business. "You shall not have in your bag differing weights, a large and a small" (Deuteronomy 25:13).

The meaning here is that the same honest and fair standard must apply to everyone equally. To use differing standards of measure would be unfair, dishonest, and unkind. In Proverbs, God expresses his abhorrence of differing weights and false scales. Godly kindness rests on truth and justice.

A just balance and scales belong to the LORD; all the weights of the bag are His concern (Proverbs 16:11).

Differing weights are an abomination to the LORD, and a false scale is not good (Proverbs 20:23).

I would even hazard to say that having different standards for behaving kindly throughout the course of the year is the same as using unjust scales. In both instances, the person's behavior serves their own selfish ambition rather than serving the need of another person in a kind, just, and honest manner.

Balanced on the Fulcrum

However, the fruit of kindness should not be administered with cavalier abandon lest it result in creating an even greater injustice than its absence presents. Who would disagree that there is no kindness in depriving your own household for the indulgence of a stranger?

But if anyone does not provide for his own, and especially for those of his household, he has denied the faith and is worse than an unbeliever (1 Timothy 5:8).

Jesus derided such disregard for one's family when he confronted the Pharisees, who favored keeping their traditions over the commandments of God. Discoursing on the fifth commandment (to honor one's parents), Jesus makes it clear that disregard for familial responsibility cannot be justified by the traditions of men. It is, in fact, the height if injustice, contrary to the truth of God's commands and flagrantly unkind.

"Neglecting the commandment of God, you hold to the tradition of men." He was also saying to them, "You are experts at setting aside the commandment of God in order to keep your tradition. For Moses said, 'Honor your father and your mother;' and, 'He who speaks evil of father or mother, is to be put to death'; but you say, 'If a man says to his father or his mother, whatever I have that would help you is Corban (that is to say, given to God),' you no longer permit him to do anything for his father or his

mother; thus invalidating the word of God by your
tradition which you have handed down; and you do
many things such as that." (Mark 7:8-13).

As we weigh kindness and justice on the fulcrum of
truth, we are commanded to do so without partiality. Moses
admonished the Israelites that they were not to show
"injustice in judgment" nor were they to "be partial to the
poor nor defer to the great, but you are to judge your
neighbor fairly" (Leviticus 19:15). James further illustrates
the importance of being impartial in our acts of kindness:

My brethren, do not hold your faith in our glorious
Lord Jesus Christ with an attitude of personal
favoritism. For if a man comes into your assembly
with a gold ring and dressed in fine clothes, and
there also comes in a poor man in dirty clothes, and
you pay special attention to the one who is wearing
the fine clothes, and say, "You sit here in a good
place," and you say to the poor man, "You stand
over there, or sit down by my footstool," have you
not made distinctions among yourselves, and
become judges with evil motives? . . .

If, however, you are fulfilling the royal law
according to the Scripture, "You shall love your
neighbor as yourself," you are doing well. But if you
show partiality, you are committing sin and are
convicted by the law as transgressors (James 2:1-9).

We must distribute the fruit of kindness without
partiality, while employing the discernment that comes
through knowing truth and acting justly.

Judaism teaches that the greatest means of charity or
kindness is to enable the poor to earn a living (Talmud:
Sabbath; Maimonides, Mishnah Torah: Laws Concerning
Gifts to the Poor 10:7-14). This brings to mind the Chinese
proverb that if you feed a man a fish, you feed him for a day;
but if you teach the man to fish, you feed him for a lifetime.

Perhaps we need to sow more seeds of long-term kindness into peoples' lives rather than short-term solutions that only serve to perpetuate their current state of affairs.

The motive behind our acts of kindness is also of concern. Jesus reminds us that when performing kind acts, we must take care in examining our hearts. In Matthew's Gospel, the Lord instructs us that when we provide for the poor, we should do so in private before God and not for recognition from men.

But when you give to the poor, do not let your left hand know what your right hand is doing, so that your giving will be in secret; and your Father who sees what is done in secret will reward you (Matthew 6.3-4).

Every true act of kindness should serve as a reminder of God's kindness to us. Consider again the winter holidays we celebrate. Christ came as a babe in obscurity to provide mankind the means of salvation. Hanukkah, the Feast of Lights, illustrates God's kindness by miraculously providing oil for the Temple Menorah, which allowed the time needed for the priests to purify a fresh supply of oil. Kindness does not enable others to remain in darkness and bondage. Instead, Godlike kindness empowers them to go free in the light of his goodness.

The beginning and end of The Law is the performance of lovingkindness (Talmud: Sotah 14a).

What is desirable in a man is his kindness, and it is better to be a poor man than a liar (Proverbs 19:22).

What have you harvested lately?

1. When do I behave most kindly to others? When am I least kind?

2. Who can I offer kindness to today?

3. What changes should I make in order to act with more kindness toward others?

4. What have I harvested lately?

A Genuine Crop
The Fruit of Goodness

But the Fruit of the Spirit is love, joy, peace, patience, kindness, goodness, faithfulness, gentleness, self-control; against such things there is no law (Galatians 5:22-23).

And He said, "I Myself will make all My goodness pass before you, and will proclaim the name of the LORD before you; and I will be gracious to whom I will be gracious, and will show compassion on whom I will show compassion" (Exodus 33:19).

The Good Word

The sixth of the fruit identified by Paul in Galatians 5 is that of goodness. Bearing the fruit of goodness has as much to do with the soil in which the seed is sown as it does with the seed itself. Referring to the parable of the sower, Mark's Gospel notes that the seed of the sower is the Word of God; "The sower sows the word" (Mark 4:14).

In 2 Timothy 2:15, we read that the Word is Truth:

Be diligent to present yourself approved to God as a workman who does not need to be ashamed, accurately handling the word of truth."

And in Hebrews 6:5 it is referred to as goodness; they have "tasted the good word of God and the powers of the age to come."

Consequently, you would naturally expect this good seed, which is the Word of God, to bring forth a rich harvest of goodness. But before counting our bushels, let's see where the seed is falling and what might be done to assure a crop of goodness and all the blessings it has in store.

A Penetrated Heart

The parable about the sower is presented in each of the first three Gospels. We looked at Matthew's depiction of the parable when we examined the fruit of love. As we discover the beauty of goodness, let's consider Luke's account of the sower and the seed:

When a large crowd was coming together, and those from the various cities were journeying to Him, He spoke by way of a parable: The sower went out to sow his seed; and as he sowed, some fell beside the road, and it was trampled under foot and the birds of the air ate it up. Other seed fell on rocky soil, and as soon as it grew up, it withered away,

*because it had no moisture. Other seed fell among
the thorns; and the thorns grew up with it and
choked it out. Other seed fell into the good soil, and
grew up, and produced a crop a hundred times as
great. . . .*

*The seed is the word of God. Those beside the road
are those who have heard; then the devil comes and
takes away the word from their heart, so that they
will not believe and be saved. Those on the rocky
soil are those who, when they hear, receive the word
with joy; and these have no firm root; they believe
for a while, and in time of temptation fall away. The
seed which fell among the thorns, these are the ones
who have heard, and as they go on their way they
are choked with worries and riches and pleasures of
this life, and bring no fruit to maturity.*

*But the seed in the good soil, these are the ones who
have heard the word in an honest and good heart,
and hold it fast, and bear fruit with perseverance*
(Luke 8:5-8, 11-15).

In the course of sowing, some of the sower's good seed
falls along the path, some on rocky ground, some among
thorns, and some on good soil. These represent the
conditions of the heart into which the seed of the Word is
sown.

The path where the seed is quickly snatched up by the
birds represents the heart that hears the Word but does not
embrace it or understand it. Consequently, the enemy steals
it away before the unsuspecting soul has a chance to reflect
further on the good seed of the Truth that bore the potential
of a great harvest.

Seed falling on the heart of rocky ground meets with
enough understanding to be embraced just long enough to
take root. But with impenetrable rock and shallow soil, the
tender green shoots quickly wither under the assault of the
sun and lack of moisture. At the first signs of ridicule,

rejection, or regret the shallow root structure gives way and what began so quickly dies just as fast. A heart that will not be penetrated will not produce a crop of goodness.

Competition is the downfall of the seed sown into the weeds and thorn bushes. These represent worldly temptations such as affluence, popularity, notoriety, and the like. Here the seed may find decent soil in which to grow, but it must fight against the infringing lusts and temptations of the world. Even if the Word does begin to take hold, all too often it is choked out and withers as the thorny heart yields in preference of what the world, rather than the Word, has to offer.

Finally we come to the good soil. Christ instructs the disciples, "And the one on whom seed was sown on the good soil, this is the man who hears the word and understands it; who indeed bears fruit and brings forth, some a hundredfold, some sixty, and some thirty" (Matthew 13:23).

If we want our personal character to bear a crop of goodness, it is necessary to prepare the soil of our hearts. We must break up the ground and remove the paths hardened by time, by hurts, by our own cynicism. The impediments, both below and above the surface of the heart, are like impenetrable rocks that prevent the seed of goodness from putting down deep roots. They must be removed.

And as for the weeds and thorn bushes that represent the temptations of the world, these must be fully uprooted, ripped up, and burned out of our lives. It is up to each one of us to prepare the soil of our temperaments to be the good soil that will receive, nurture, cultivate, and yield a bountiful harvest of goodness.

Trees and Temperament

Christ warns, "Either make the tree good and its fruit good, or make the tree bad and its fruit bad; for the tree is known by its fruit" (Matthew 12:33). If the goal is to grow a good tree yielding good fruit, then the soil must be properly prepared. There is no option of being somewhere in the middle.

Think about the last time you bit into a piece of fruit that wasn't rotten, but it wasn't flavorful either. It was just a sorry disappointment to your taste buds. Chances are you didn't bother taking a second bite. Instead you probably threw it out not bothering to taste any more.

Christ had the same response to a congregation of believers who had allowed themselves to become absolutely mediocre. He threatened to spit them out if they didn't change their ways, repair their character and become either get hot or cold:

> *I know your deeds, that you are neither cold nor hot; I wish that you were cold or hot. So because you are lukewarm, and neither hot nor cold, I will spit you out of My mouth.*

> *Because you say, "I am rich, and have become wealthy, and have need of nothing," and you do not know that you are wretched and miserable and poor and blind and naked, I advise you to buy from Me gold refined by fire so that you may become rich, and white garments so that you may clothe yourself, and that the shame of your nakedness will not be revealed; and eye salve to anoint your eyes so that you may see (Revelation 3:15-18).*

Moral Responsibility

Let's consider for a moment the descriptive terms used in this passage. Referring to their character, Jesus depicts this congregation as wretched, miserable, poor, blind and naked. Such traits are displeasing to our Lord.

Instead, we should cast of wretchedness and become distinguished by exhibiting Christ nature. Rather than being miserable, we should be content. If our character is poor and morally bankrupt, we need to invest ourselves in morality. And if we find ourselves naked we must humbly seek to be robed in Christ's own righteousness.

Just as the congregation at Laodicea was responsible for their moral character, so are we. We must choose to live our lives abounding in goodness which springs from the good seed sown into the soil of our hearts. But what exactly is this fruit of goodness? Paul provides insights for us in Ephesians 5:8-11:

> For you were formerly darkness, but now you are Light in the Lord; walk as children of Light (for the fruit of the Light consists in all goodness and righteousness and truth), trying to learn what is pleasing to the Lord. Do not participate in the unfruitful deeds of darkness, but instead even expose them.

Goodness and Light

We see then that goodness is associated with light, righteousness, and truth. Goodness participates in proving what is pleasing to God. It does not fellowship with works of darkness such as the hardened path, the impenetrable rocky soil, or the weed and thorn-covered ground.

Instead, goodness seeks to repair the unfit soil so that the seed of goodness may find ground there just as it has in the good soil. Notice also that the fruit of light, of which goodness is a part, is to expose the unfruitful works of darkness.

The fruit reveals the tree, the tree reveals the soil and the soil ultimately reveals the human heart. What soil have you chosen? What is the condition of your tree? What fruit are you bearing? How will the Lord judge your harvest?

We found in our examination of kindness that Paul used the Greek word *chrastotas* (χρηστότησ), which can also be translated as goodness. But for the fruit of goodness, Paul used the word *agathosuna* (ἀγαθωσύνη). Goodness, agathosuna, describes the temperament of the person performing acts of kindness, chrastotas.

So we see goodness as a fruit reflecting our own character, and which, like good soil, enables us to bear the equally good fruit of kindness with which we are able to bless others.

> *Blessed is the man who trusts in the LORD And whose trust is the LORD. For he will be like a tree planted by the water, that extends its roots by a stream and will not fear when the heat comes; but its leaves will be green, and it will not be anxious in a year of drought nor cease to yield fruit* (Jeremiah 17:7-8).

What have you harvested lately?

1. How much does my character reflect the goodness of God?

2. For whom have I demonstrated kindness out of the goodness of my heart?

3. What can I do to develop more goodness in my character?

4. What have I harvested lately?

A Sustaining Crop

The Fruit of Faithfulness

But the Fruit of the Spirit is love, joy, peace, patience, kindness, goodness, faithfulness, gentleness, self-control; against such things there is no law (Galatians 5:22-23).

Trust in the LORD and do good; dwell in the land and cultivate faithfulness (Psalm 37:3).

Wary of Wadis

There was a time when a person's word and handshake were sufficient assurance for a contract or agreement. Unfortunately, such behavior has all but disappeared. An even greater misfortune is that this lack of faithfulness is nearly as evident among Believers as it is in the world at large. Such circumstances should give each of us pause as we consider how much faithfulness our own lives exhibit. Are you producing the fruit of faithfulness in your daily walk or are you proving yourself to be faithless? When you give your word, are you committed to fulfilling what you have promised, whether to God or to man?

Job had the misfortune of experiencing firsthand the faithlessness of his supposed friends. In Job 6:15-18, he likens his friends to a desert wadi.

My brothers have acted deceitfully like a wadi, like the torrents of wadis which vanish, which are turbid because of ice and into which the snow melts. When they become waterless, they are silent, when it is hot, they vanish from their place. The paths of their course wind along, they go up into nothing and perish.

A wadi is a ravine or small canyon susceptible to flash flooding. Anyone traveling to Israel becomes quite familiar with this geological feature of the terrain. In some seasons, travelers may find that a desert wadi is abounding with life-giving water. In other seasons, the wadi remains dry and only taunts the weary traveler with the promise of water, while yielding nothing but dust and dirt.

The caravans of Tema looked, the travelers of Sheba hoped for [the wadis]. They were disappointed for they had trusted, they came there and were confounded. Indeed, you have now become such [wadis] (Job 6:19-20).

Like the wadis, Job's friends came with the refreshing promise of friendship that comforts and soothes the weary. However, instead of providing refreshment they proved to be disappointments, bringing with them only contempt and disdain.

Job was desperate for consolation and encouragement. His soul was withering like a man lost in the wilderness. He looked with a hopeful heart to his friends. Even as they drew near to him, they gave the impression they would faithfully provide the revitalizing solace of fellowship he so desperately desired. Instead, they were like dry and dusty wadis, bringing Job nothing more than additional condemnation and heartache. As friends they proved themselves to be faithless.

How blessed we are that our Heavenly Father is not like a desert wadi. Instead, Scripture likens him to an ever-flowing stream of living water.

O LORD, the hope of Israel, all who forsake You will be put to shame. Those who turn away on earth will be written down, because they have forsaken the fountain of living water, even the LORD (Jeremiah 17:13).

Living Waters

Unlike man, God remains faithful at all times. Writing to Timothy, Paul encourages his protégé concerning God's faithfulness with these words: "If we are faithless, He remains faithful, for He cannot deny Himself" (1 Timothy 2:13). Likewise, King David understood the faithfulness of the Lord and wrote:

Your lovingkindness, O LORD, extends to the heavens, Your faithfulness reaches to the skies. . . They drink their fill of the abundance of Your house; and You give them to drink of the river of Your delights. For with You is the fountain of life; in Your light we see light (Psalm 36:5, 8-9).

David was a man well acquainted with the wilderness and the desert. He knew firsthand the need for life-giving water in barren lands. How eloquently he likens this need to the need of spiritual refreshment. Just as a desert spring continually brings life from the rocks, so God's spring of faithfulness brings life to our barren souls.

It is this kind of faithfulness that Paul instructs us to propagate in our lives. We are to follow our Lord's example of faithfulness so that we bring refreshment to others rather than the bitterness of disappointment.

It is a trustworthy statement . . . If we are faithless, He remains faithful, for He cannot deny Himself (2 Timothy 2:11-13).

We are not to be like morning clouds that promise rain and then pass beyond the horizon without shedding so much as a drop of moisture. Hosea likens ancient Judah's faithlessness to such clouds:

For your loyalty is like a morning cloud and like the dew which goes away early" (Hosea 6:4).

God's response to such faithlessness was judgment on the nation. Similarly, Jesus cursed the fig tree for not being faithful to produce its early crop of fruit, the breba crop that we discussed in the chapter on the fruit of joy. Speaking to the barren fig tree Jesus said:

"No longer shall there ever be any fruit from you."
And at once the fig tree withered (Matthew 21.18-19).

Truly there are consequences for producing faithfulness or faithlessness in one's life. Unlike fruitless fig trees or an unpredictable wadi, we are to faithfully produce the Fruit of the Spirit in season and out of season.

Oh that God's people would walk in such faithfulness which should be as an ever flowing spring of life giving water.

Preach the word; be ready in season and out of season; reprove, rebuke, exhort, with great patience and instruction (2 Timothy 4:2).

Proverbs instructs us concerning the faithful and the faithless:

Like the cold of snow in the time of harvest is a faithful messenger to those who send him, for he refreshes the soul of his masters. Like clouds and wind without rain is a man who boasts of his gifts falsely (Proverbs 25:13-14).

And Isaiah describes God's faithfulness for us, giving us a clear example to follow. God's faithfulness is depicted as a "spring of water whose waters do not fail" (Isaiah 58:11). The result of such faithfulness is refreshment to the soul and strength to one's bones. It does not disappoint.

Form or Function

Conversely, faithlessness merits the Lord's disapproval and curries his judgment. Isaiah reports the Lord's opinion of such behavior:

Because this people draw near with their words and honor Me with their lip service, but they remove their hearts far from Me, and their reverence for Me consists of tradition learned by rote, therefore behold, I will once again deal marvelously with this people, wondrously marvelous; and the wisdom of their wise men will perish, and the discernment of their discerning men will be concealed.

Woe to those who deeply hide their plans from the LORD, and whose deeds are done in a dark place,

and they say, "Who sees us?" or "Who knows us?"
(Isaiah 29:13-15).

Paul warns Timothy to avoid such people, who give the appearance of being faithful, but in reality are not. We are admonished to avoid people who hold to a form of godliness, while denying the function of its power (2 Timothy 3:5). A dry streambed, like a faithless friend, brings disappointment and destruction.

If we live in faithfulness to the Lord our God, faithfulness to others should naturally be a part of our character. Conversely, if we fail to show faithfulness to others, we must question whether we are truly being faithful to God.

Since faithfulness, as with each Fruit of the Spirit, flows from agape love, the admonition of the Apostle John concerning our love for God aptly applies to faithfulness as well:

If someone says, "I love God," and hates his brother, he is a liar; for the one who does not love his brother whom he has seen, cannot love God whom he has not seen (1 John 4:20).

In other words, if we are not faithful to the people we do see, are we honestly behaving faithfully to God whom we do not see?

Be encouraged, therefore, to be a faithful spring and not an unreliable wadi. Don't offer the promise of faithfulness without giving the gift of faithfulness. Don't raise hopes of encouragement, only to bring discouragement. With your promise, to man and to God, give the thing promised. Bear the fruit of faithfulness toward others, just as our God has shown his faithfulness to us.

O love the LORD, all you His godly ones! The LORD preserves the faithful and fully recompenses the proud doer (Psalm 31:23).

What have you harvested lately?

1. How faithful am I in consistently serving God?

2. When do I behave with faithfulness toward my family, friends, and coworkers? When don't I?

3. How can I become more like a faithful stream rather than an unreliable wadi?

4. What have I harvested lately?

A Tender Crop
The Fruit of Gentleness

But the Fruit of the Spirit is love, joy, peace, patience, kindness, goodness, faithfulness, gentleness, self-control; against such things there is no law (Galatians 5:22-23).

You have also given me the shield of Your salvation, and Your right hand upholds me; And Your gentleness makes me great (Psalm 18:35).

Humble Fortitude

Opportunities to demonstrate the fruit of gentleness abound in daily life. Unfortunately, modern society does not often value this character trait except when extended to children, the elderly, the disadvantaged, or the infirm. Yet the Apostle Paul places no such limitations on producing the fruit of gentleness in one's life. Followers of Jesus Christ are to make the most of every opportunity to demonstrate gentleness to others. As Paul says, against such behavior there is no law.

The opportunity to demonstrate gentleness through constraint is generally missed today. Modern society tends to esteem the superiority of strength above all, and conditions us to think of gentleness as a weak response. Such a belief stems from the Darwinian principle of the survival of the fittest. In society, this quickly devolves into *might makes right* which culminates in dictatorial abuse.

However, this notion that gentleness is synonymous with weakness could not be further from the truth. Consider, for example, Moses. This is the man God chose to deliver Israel from the oppression of slavery and servitude in Egypt.

Moses was undaunted in the presence of Pharaoh and his court. He was unflinching when confronting the rebelliousness of the people he led. He entered the very presence of God confidently, even daring to dissuade the Almighty from his plan to destroy his chosen people. Truly Moses was a man of great strength. Yet the source of his strength was anything but conventional by modern standards.

In Numbers 12:3, Moses is described as being "very humble, more than any man who was on the face of the earth." How is it, then, that this man of such immense strength and fortitude is described as being meek, being gentle, being humble?

USC professor of special education and counseling, Leo Buscaglia, has been quoted as saying, "Gentleness can only be expected from the strong." Chinese author Han Suyin similarly proposed, "There is nothing stronger in the world than gentleness." Could it be true that the greater one's capacity for strength, the more profound one's demonstration of gentleness is? Certainly we see in the life of Moses that his capacity for gentleness directly impacted the greatness of his strength.

Juxtapositions

I am reminded of a photograph by Anne Geddes. Perhaps you have seen it. The photo is in black and white, showing a close-up of rugged and gnarled, masculine hands cradling a tiny infant. It is a profoundly touching depiction of gentleness.

Had the hands holding the infant been those of a young mother, the image would not have portrayed the stark contrast of strength and tenderness. The image clearly evokes the sentiment that to be truly gentle, one must be truly strong.

What opportunities present themselves to you that may appear to call for strength but would be better served by the constraint of gentleness? Do you possess strength like Moses but fail to seize opportunities to wield that strength through a gentle word or a meek response?

Other opportunities for demonstrating gentleness occur in the form of confrontations. Here are opportunities to be gentle and diffuse contention and strife. Surely it is not unacceptable to defend oneself when unjustly offended, is it? But then does one truly bear spiritual fruit by being gentle only to those who are gentle toward us? What example did Christ give when in such situations?

Paul refers to the meekness and gentleness of Jesus in 2 Corinthians 10:1. He writes, "I, Paul, myself urge you by the meekness and gentleness of Christ." This gentleness and meekness are also depicted in Isaiah's prophecy concerning Christ's crucifixion. The prophet compares the Savior's gentleness in the face of his accusers to a mute lamb being led to slaughter:

> *He was oppressed and He was afflicted, yet He did not open His mouth; like a lamb that is led to slaughter, and like a sheep that is silent before its shearers, so He did not open His mouth* (Isaiah 53:7).

Proverbs similarly admonishes that a gentle response is more effective in a confrontation than a harsh one. "A gentle answer turns away wrath, But a harsh word stirs up anger" (Proverbs 15:1).

It is in the juxtaposed power and meekness of the Cross that we truly see our Lord's character. If he exhibited gentleness in the midst of his agonizing battle over sin and death, shouldn't we likewise in the strength of gentleness and meekness when we confront opposition and persecution? In Matthew's Gospel, Christ instructs us not only to love those who love us, but to love our enemies as well.

> *You have heard that it was said, "You shall love your neighbor and hate your enemy." But I say to you, love your enemies and pray for those who persecute you, so that you may be sons of your Father who is in heaven; for He causes His sun to rise on the evil and the good, and sends rain on the righteous and the unrighteous.*
>
> *"For if you love those who love you, what reward do you have? Do not even the tax collectors do the same? If you greet only your brothers, what more are you doing than others? Do not even the Gentiles do the same? Therefore you are to be perfect, as your heavenly Father is perfect* (Matthew 5:43-48).

What is said of love can equally be applied to gentleness. If you only show gentleness to the gentle, you have missed the opportunity to diffuse strife and contention. The opportunity is also lost for showing that Christ came to love, be gentle toward, and reconcile the undeserving. He first loved us and showed his gentleness toward us while we were yet sinners.

But God demonstrates his own love toward us, in that while we were yet contending with Him through our sinful nature, Christ died for us (Romans 5:8).

Unexpected Compassion

Showing gentleness to those who least expect it leaves indelible marks of love on a person's soul. Profound impressions are made when we respond with gentleness toward those with whom we may typically have a contentious relationship.

Consider, for instance, the tension that existed between the Jews and Samaritans of Jesus' day. Because of the guile each group had long held for the other, neither would have expected the other to treat it with gentleness.

The man beaten by thieves and left for dead on the road to Jericho, had he been conscious, would never have expected to be treated gently with compassion by a Samaritan.

Jesus replied and said, "A man was going down from Jerusalem to Jericho, and fell among robbers, and they stripped him and beat him, and went away leaving him half dead. And by chance a priest was going down on that road, and when he saw him, he passed by on the other side. Likewise a Levite also, when he came to the place and saw him, passed by on the other side.

But a Samaritan, who was on a journey, came upon him; and when he saw him, he felt compassion, and came to him and bandaged up his wounds, pouring oil and wine on them; and he put him on his own beast, and brought him to an inn and took care of him.

On the next day he took out two denarii and gave them to the innkeeper and said, 'Take care of him; and whatever more you spend, when I return I will repay you.' Which of these three do you think proved to be a neighbor to the man who fell into the robbers' hands?" And he said, "The one who showed mercy toward him." Then Jesus said to him, "Go and do the same" (Luke 10:30-37).

Jews in that day had little to no interaction with Samaritans. The victim in the story would have certainly expected his fellow Jews, the Levite, and the priest, to assist him—but certainly not a Samaritan. The unexpected gentleness, compassion, and provision from the hand of this stranger serves to magnify the tender care of one man's actions toward the other.

Gracious Fortitude

Another illustration comes to us from the life of David, as told in 1 Samuel 25. It centers on the actions of Abigail, the wife of a foolish man named Nabal. After Nabal rudely refused David's request of hospitality, a common practice throughout Middle Eastern culture both then and now, the young king was ready to eradicate Nabal and his household.

Realizing the dire consequences of her husband's behavior, Abigail took the matter into her own hands. She might have considered approaching David rashly or defiantly in light of what he intended. However, Abigail was a wise woman. Therefore, she approached the King with a gentle and humble spirit, requesting that her household be spared and providing from her own hand provisions for the King and his mighty men.

> *But one of the young men told Abigail, Nabal's wife, saying, "Behold, David sent messengers from the wilderness to greet our master, and he scorned them. Yet the men were very good to us, and we were not insulted, nor did we miss anything as long as we went about with them, while we were in the fields."* (1 Samuel 14-15)

Abigail was faced with several options at this point. She could stand back and let Nabal get what he had coming. She could rail against David for his vindictiveness. Or, she could put the needs of her household above any desire she may have for retribution and seek to serve rather than be served. Scripture informs us that Abigail chose well.

> *Then Abigail hurried and took two hundred loaves of bread and two jugs of wine and five sheep already prepared and five measures of roasted grain and a hundred clusters of raisins and two hundred cakes of figs, and loaded them on donkeys. . . .*

> *When Abigail saw David, she hurried and dismounted from her donkey, and fell on her face before David and bowed herself to the ground. She fell at his feet and said,*

> *"On me alone, my lord, be the blame. And please let your maidservant speak to you, and listen to the words of your maidservant. . . . Now therefore, my lord, as the LORD lives, and as your soul lives, since the LORD has restrained you from shedding blood, and from avenging yourself by your own hand, now then let your enemies and those who seek evil against my lord, be as Nabal. . . . And when the LORD does for my lord according to all the good that He has spoken concerning you, and appoints you ruler over Israel, this will not cause grief or a troubled heart to my lord, both by having shed blood*

without cause and by my lord having avenged himself. When the LORD deals well with my lord, then remember your maidservant" (1 Samuel 25:18-31).

By responding with a gentle and kind hand, Abigail spared her household from certain death and managed to provide for the needs of David and his men. Beyond that, her gentle response in a volatile situation prevented David from having the burden of Nabal's blood on his hands.

Abigail did not come groveling to David. She did not come to him with resentful appeasement. She did not behave with anger or defiance. Instead, she approached David with grace, fortitude and a gentle hand that ultimately kept the peace and supplied his and his companions' needs.

This unexpected service defused David's anger and allowed God, not the King, to punish Abigail's foolish and selfish husband. In addition to saving the lives of her household, Abigail was personally rewarded for her gentleness and wisdom by later becoming wife to King David.

Meek and Joyful

Just as an unexpected cool rain shower on a hot summer day brings refreshment, so gentleness refreshes the soul when proffered to those who least expect it. Are you looking for opportunities to extend the blessing of gentleness to those who do not anticipate it from your hand?

Opportunities to demonstrate gentleness are everywhere. It may be in the strength of gentle constraint, in the diffusing gentleness of a reconciling tone, or in the compassionate expression of gentleness to one who least expects it. Whatever the opportunity, those who bear the fruit of gentleness are promised to inherit the earth.

Blessed are the gentle, for they shall inherit the earth (Matthew 5:5).

But perhaps the more enticing benefit for behaving gently is to receive fresh joy from the Lord himself:

The meek shall obtain fresh joy in the Lord, and the poor among mankind shall exult in the Holy One of Israel (Isaiah 29:19 ESV).

What have you harvested lately?

1. When have I responded with gentleness to someone who did not expect it?

2. How does the gentle behavior of another person affect me?

3. In what areas of my life should I demonstrate more gentleness?

4. What have I harvested lately?

A Reasonable Crop

The Fruit of Self-Control

But the Fruit of the Spirit is love, joy, peace, patience, kindness, goodness, faithfulness, gentleness, self-control; against such things there is no law (Galatians 5:22-23).

Everyone who competes in the games exercises self-control in all things. They then do it to receive a perishable wreath, but we an imperishable (1 Corinthians 9:25).

Constrained to Serve

In the verses preceding the Apostle Paul's listing of spiritual
fruit in Galatians chapter 5, we read his admonition to the
Galatians adjuring them not to succumb to over exuberant
attempts to serve God:

> It was for freedom that Christ set us free; therefore
> keep standing firm and do not be subject again to a
> yoke of slavery.
>
> Behold I, Paul, say to you that if you receive
> circumcision, Christ will be of no benefit to you. And
> I testify again to every man who receives
> circumcision, that he is under obligation to keep the
> whole Law. You have been severed from Christ, you
> who are seeking to be justified by law; you have
> fallen from grace.
>
> For we through the Spirit, by faith, are waiting for
> the hope of righteousness. For in Christ Jesus
> neither circumcision nor uncircumcision means
> anything, but faith working through love.
>
> You were running well; who hindered you from
> obeying the truth? This persuasion did not come
> from Him who calls you. A little leaven leavens the
> whole lump of dough. I have confidence in you in the
> Lord that you will adopt no other view; but the one
> who is disturbing you will bear his judgment,
> whoever he is.
>
> But I, brethren, if I still preach circumcision, why
> am I still persecuted? Then the stumbling block of
> the cross has been abolished. I wish that those who
> are troubling you would even mutilate themselves.
>
> For you were called to freedom, brethren; only do
> not turn your freedom into an opportunity for the

flesh, but through love serve one another (Galatians 5:1-13).

In this passage Paul particularly warns the Galatians of being seduced by the Judaizers, those who insisted that to be truly righteous, a man must be circumcised. Paul counters that man cannot add one thing to the righteousness purchased by Christ in his blood on the cross. Righteousness, which is to say salvation, is obtained through faith in the atoning sacrifice of Jesus' death and resurrection.

Given this backdrop and Paul's admonition that the Fruit of the Spirit are grounded in love, we need to give contextual consideration to the list of spiritual fruit and their relevance to the Galatians in particular, and then to all Christians in general.

Paul did not pen this list of spiritual fruit in isolation. By understanding better his reasons for writing these things to the Galatian believers, we will better understand how and why we should seek to bear these fruit in our own lives.

But the Fruit of the Spirit is love, joy, peace, patience, kindness, goodness, faithfulness, gentleness, self-control; against such things there is no law (Galatians 5:22-23).

Cardinal Virtue

To grasp more clearly the nature of the nine Fruit of the Spirit, we begin by considering the first and last entries on Paul's list. Love is the first fruit, the starting point. This is a sensible beginning, since it is impractical, if not impossible, to produce the fruit of joy, peace, patience, kindness, goodness, faithfulness, gentleness, or self-control apart from love. Without the motivation of agape love, the other fruit wither and waste away.

What enables a person to behave kindly when being ill-treated other than unconditional agape love? Why would a person choose to be patient with others when feeling stressed or overwhelmed if not for unconditional love? Love is the foundation upon which the other fruit rest. Indeed, it is only through agape love that we may sincerely serve one another (Galatians 5:13).

If agape love is then by necessity the first of the fruit, why has Paul chosen to complete his list of spiritual fruit with self-control?

The Greek word translated as self-control is *egkrataia* (ἐγκράτεια) a term esteemed by Socrates as being a cardinal virtue. The term pertains to self-restraint and self-discipline. Paul uses it in 1 Corinthians 9:25 when he speaks of Christ's followers being like runners who compete in a race, exercising self-control in order to receive the imperishable crown of righteousness and eternal life:

> *Do you not know that those who run in a race all run, but only one receives the prize? Run in such a way that you may win. Everyone who competes in the games exercises self-control in all things. They then do it to receive a perishable wreath, but we an imperishable* (1 Corinthians 9:24-25).

Bounty within Boundaries

This self-control or self-discipline has also been referred to as temperance or chastity. But to portray this fruit as only exercising control over one's appetites falls short of its true significance. As with love, self-control is understood best by considering it in combination with the other fruit. By exercising self-control, one is able to practice the other Fruit of the Spirit in proper balance.

Balance and order are critical to the appropriate behavior of congregations. Speaking again to the church at Corinth, Paul has this to say:

*What is the outcome then, brethren? When you
assemble, each one has a psalm, has a teaching, has
a revelation, has a tongue, has an interpretation. Let
all things be done for edification. . . But all things
must be done properly and in an orderly manner*
(1 Corinthians 14:26, 40)

This fruit of self-discipline prevents us from going out-of-bounds when practicing joy, or faithfulness, or gentleness, or any of the other fruit. Remember that Paul is instructing the Galatians to avoid excess in their Christian walk. In their exuberance to serve Christ, he does not want them to be caught up in religiosity—such as submitting, merely for religious purposes, to circumcision, or to worshiping on a particular day, or to eating only certain foods.

By instructing them to begin their spiritual service in agape love and to conclude it with temperance, he assists them in propagating a bumper crop of excellent, untainted spiritual fruit. Otherwise, they run the risk of only having the appearance of godliness while undermining the power of true God-likeness (2 Timothy 3:5).

Self-control consists of two primary elements. The first is self-discipline, which assures that we practice those things that are good and righteous while abstaining from those behaviors that are immoral or offensive. The second is that of temperance.

By exercising temperance, we are less likely to overindulge whether in a good thing or in something bad. By exercising self-discipline we will not neglect to show godly love and concern for our neighbor. Likewise, the temperance of self-control will assure that such affection is not shown unbounded. For unbound affection, even though it begins as agape, if left undisciplined, may erupt into lust or immoral passion.

And so it is with each of the Fruit of the Spirit. Self-control assures that the righteous person is disciplined to bear spiritual fruit for the blessing and benefit of others, while also preventing such a practice from becoming excessive.

Joy should not become so extreme that it dissolves into frivolous naiveté. Peace need not be so uninformed that it becomes blind pacifism. Patience need not be so unending that it results in injustice. Kindness should not be so unrestricted that it becomes foolishness. Goodness need not be so unrestrained that it results in a lack of discernment. Faithfulness should not be unquestioned lest it be reduced to a loss of discretion. And gentleness need not become passive vulnerability by losing the temperance of assertiveness.

When practiced without boundaries, the Fruit of the Spirit can lead to error just as the Galatians' unbound desire for righteousness led them back into the bondage of works. Although their motivation toward righteousness was commendable, their efforts toward the goal became self-reliant rather than self-disciplined. Paul instructs them as a caring mentor to practice those things that lead to righteousness and to avoid those things that encumber their spiritual walk.

Temperance and Salt

If it seems contrary to the nature of Christ to place limitations on the fruit we bear, consider the parable of the ten virgins:

Then the kingdom of heaven will be comparable to ten virgins, who took their lamps and went out to meet the bridegroom. Five of them were foolish, and five were prudent. For when the foolish took their lamps, they took no oil with them, but the prudent took oil in flasks along with their lamps.

Now while the bridegroom was delaying, they all got drowsy and began to sleep.

But at midnight there was a shout, "Behold, the bridegroom! Come out to meet him." Then all those virgins rose and trimmed their lamps. The foolish said to the prudent, "Give us some of your oil, for our lamps are going out." But the prudent answered, "No, there will not be enough for us and you too; go instead to the dealers and buy some for yourselves."

And while they were going away to make the purchase, the bridegroom came, and those who were ready went in with him to the wedding feast; and the door was shut.

Later the other virgins also came, saying, "Lord, lord, open up for us." But he answered, "Truly I say to you, I do not know you." Be on the alert then, for you do not know the day nor the hour (Matthew 25:1-13).

Of the ten, only five had the foresight to plan ahead for their provisions in the event that the bridegroom should arrive later than expected. After a prolonged delay, he finally arrived and the five foolish virgins asked their prudent companions to show them the kindness of sharing their oil. The response was *No.*

The wise women reasoned that if they shared their oil, all ten would run out and none would be able to find the way to the wedding feast. The five wise virgins suggested that the five women who lacked oil for their lamps go and purchase their own supply.

This seemingly unkind behavior was not depicted as such by our Lord. Instead, he used it as an example of how to temper kindness with self-control, and thereby uphold the accountability of each one for her own preparedness or lack thereof.

Self-control, temperance, prudence, self-discipline—do these describe a Fruit of the Spirit to be exercised apart from the other fruit? Perhaps not. Perhaps self-control, like love, is intimately and necessarily intertwined in each of the other fruit. Perhaps self-control is listed with the fruit for the purpose of assuring that all the fruit remain wholesome and untainted by excess.

Just as salt is, by itself, flavorful, so it is with the benefits of practicing self-control. Yet temperance and salt are best enjoyed when applied to other morsels. As salt brings out all that is savory in the meal, so self-control brings out all that is most excellent in the fruit that we bear.

I, wisdom, dwell with prudence, and I find knowledge and discretion (Proverbs 8:12).

What have you harvested lately?

1. How self-disciplined am I in producing the Fruit of the Spirit?

2. What area of my life would most benefit from a greater level of self-control?

3. How much more could I serve Christ and others by exhibiting more godly discretion in my life?

4. What have I harvested lately?

Reaping the Harvest

But the Fruit of the Spirit is love, joy, peace, patience, kindness, goodness, faithfulness, gentleness, self-control; against such things there is no law (Galatians 5:22-23).

Return to the Vineyard

Let's return to the grower of the un-harvested vineyard we met in our opening chapter. Although reluctant to reap the harvest that was so well tended, this tiller of the soil could teach us yet one more simple but crucial truth.

If grapevines are cultivated, the harvest yields grapes. If tomato seeds are planted in tidy rows, a bounty of tomatoes is grown. If the pastures are sown with barley, lush bales are gathered for the livestock come fall. It really should be self-evident. Whatever a person plants, that is what is reaped.

Do not be deceived, God is not mocked; for whatever a man sows, this he will also reap. For the one who sows to his own flesh will from the flesh reap corruption, but the one who sows to the Spirit will from the Spirit reap eternal life.

Let us not lose heart in doing good, for in due time we will reap if we do not grow weary. So then, while we have opportunity, let us do good to all people, and especially to those who are of the household of the faith (Galatians 6:7-10).

What Have You Harvested Lately?

This then becomes our challenge. What is it that we are sowing in our own lives? When we sow the seed of the Spirit's Fruit in our lives, that is what we harvest. Conversely, if we sow the seeds of fleshly desire, our lives abound with corruption. Before describing the lush Fruit of the Spirit, Paul first warns us of the unsavory weeds that sprout from cultivating carnal passions:

Now the deeds of the flesh are evident, which are: immorality, impurity, sensuality, idolatry, sorcery, enmities, strife, jealousy, outbursts of anger, disputes, dissensions, factions, envying, drunkenness, carousing, and things like these, of which I forewarn you, just as I have forewarned you, that those who practice such things will not inherit the kingdom of God (Galatians 5:19-21).

Our lives boldly proclaim to all around us the type of seed we have sown. If you are harvesting more impurity than goodness, check your seed. Perhaps your days are filled with more disputes than peace. If so, check your seed. Do you exhibit more strife and jealousy than kindness and goodness? If your harvest isn't to your liking, check your seed. What have you harvested lately?

But prove yourselves doers of the word, and not merely hearers who delude themselves. For if anyone is a hearer of the word and not a doer, he is like a man who looks at his natural face in a mirror; for once he has looked at himself and gone away, he has immediately forgotten what kind of person he was.

But one who looks intently at the perfect law, the law of liberty, and abides by it, not having become a forgetful hearer but an effectual doer, this man will be blessed in what he does.

If anyone thinks himself to be religious, and yet does not bridle his tongue but deceives his own heart, this man's religion is worthless. Pure and undefiled religion in the sight of our God and Father is this: to visit orphans and widows in their distress, and to keep oneself unstained by the world (James 1:22-27).

Sustained and Nourished

It is time for each one of us to examine our hearts, our words, our actions, and the fruit that our lives are producing. The old expression, *Saying don't make it so!* applies well to the course of our lives. It is not enough to confess that we believe in Christ or that we believe the Word of God is true.

In order to reap a harvest of Spiritual Fruit that blesses our God and others, we must be active, persistent doers of God's Word. For when we act in accordance with the Word, we sow the seeds of his Spirit in our lives. And when those seeds spring to life, they produce the Fruit of the Spirit.

Don't be like the incongruous gardener we met earlier. Don't cultivate only to serve yourself. Instead, bountifully sow the truth of God's Word in your life so that your harvest is likewise bountiful. As you abundantly bear the Fruit of the Spirit, it will sustain you and nourish those you touch with the true agape love of Jesus Christ.

Now this I say, he who sows sparingly will also reap sparingly, and he who sows bountifully will also reap bountifully (1 Corinthians 9:6).

What have you harvested lately?

1. What have I harvested lately in my personal life?

2. What have I harvested lately in my relationships with people?

3. What have I harvested lately in my relationship with God?

4. What will I do now to improve my spiritual crop cultivation?

About the Author

Lori Gracey is founder and president of Branches in the Vine, an on-line ministry providing Scriptural insights and teaching. Lori holds a Master's degree in Communication from the University of California, Davis and a Bachelor's degree in English from Oral Roberts University in addition to being a lifelong student of the Bible.

The goal and ministry of Branches in the Vine is to instruct and encourage followers of Jesus Christ to abide in him so that their hearts, words and lifestyles reflect Christ to the world and in so doing bear the Fruit of the Spirit in all areas of life.

A native of Northern California, Lori now makes her home near Tulsa, Oklahoma where she also works as a business consultant and teaches Christian Worldview at Grace School of Ministry.

Visit www.BranchesInTheVine.org to read more of Lori's writing and to participate in the Branches on-line community. To order books or to schedule Lori for speaking engagements, contact her through the website or at Lori@BranchesInTheVine.org.